Sheltered Again

Sheltered Again

A Motivational Uplifting true story

Denorval Parks

authorHOUSE®

AuthorHouse™ LLC
1663 Liberty Drive
Bloomington, IN 47403
www.authorhouse.com
Phone: 1-800-839-8640

Published by AuthorHouse   05/21/2014

ISBN: 978-1-4918-7059-4 (sc)
ISBN: 978-1-4918-7052-5 (hc)
ISBN: 978-1-4918-7058-7 (e)

Library of Congress Control Number: 2014904382

This book is dedicated to all the confused and homeless people (especially homeless teens) in the world; who have goals in mind, and those who are frustrated in our upside down life.

Table of Content

ABOUT THE AUTHOR

DENORVAL PARKS IS A GIFTED INDIVIDUAL IN MANY WAYS. HE WROTE THIS BOOK AS A FORM OF THERAPY AND HOPES TO HELP OTHERS WHO HAVE A HARD TIME DEALING WITH THE PRESSURES OF LIFE. HE IS A LOVING FATHER OF THREE YOUNG MEN HE RAISED AS INFANTS AND IS LEARNING HOW TO HANDLE THE UPS AND DOWNS OF LIFE ALONG THE WAY. HE IS EXTREAMLY CONCERNED ABOUT THE FUTURE OF OUR YOUTH IN AMERICA (AND THE WORLD), AND HOPES THAT THIS BOOK CAN SOME HOW HELP THEM TO COPE WITH THE TURNMOIL THAT THEY STRUGGLE WITH DAILY, AS HE HIMSELF CONTINUES TO BE A STUDENT IN LIFE. USING WHAT HE FINDS THAT WORKS AND DOES'NT WORK IN ORDER TO CONTINUE TO KEEP HIM AFLOAT, AND HOPES IT MAY WORK FOR OTHERS AS WELL. HIS CONCERNS ARE TO MAKE A DIFFERENCE IN OUR AILING WORLD.

Introduction

I wrote this book because; I wanted to make a difference in people's lives who find life's problems to be a bit overwhelming, and difficult to deal with. Particularly people within the shelter and those who are homeless down and out, and feel that being without a home to be a dead end in their lives

Those who's self-esteem and inner core is about to explode, from life's day-to-day challenges which they find to be extremely intolerable. For people who may have the desire to do but need that push, and the encouragement needed to get over their mental hump. To get the start and momentum they need to get on the right track towards doing something with their lives that has been probably temporarily side tracked.

Many who want to move forward but don't quit have the know how or strength to do. Those who are not as-strong-as others, for whatever reason (born with a certain type of character or, unfortunately raised in a particular manner that affected them mentally for the worst), these types of wonderful people need and are crying for help in dealing with their unfortunate dilemma that's holding them back. And I want these people to know that anything is possible as-long-as you have the Lord in your heart and soul, you can get through anything, as-long-as you force yourself to be positive (if being positive is your goal) which comes in time, with practice and love for yourself. Me being homeless in the shelter (around angry people) and sleeping in the streets helped me develope the power, knowledge and know how to cope, and deal with the force of life's unfairness. As I was determined not to fold and belly over from the pressures of the unfortunate that can be dealt to all of us, which can be a difficult task to take on, but with the Lord thy God and positive thinking, combined with, the will to do, and patients, there isn't anything on earth that cannot be achieved, the only thing is that you must want to do it. I hope that what I learned and experienced over the years that worked for me can work for you, and guide you towards a positive stress free way of thinking, good luck my brother . . . I have love for you!

Chapter 1

Once Upon a time

The Shelter System . . . where's its starting point? I don't think that is a common question! People really don't care as-long-as they have a roof over their heads for themselves and their family. As-long-as they're not closing their eyes at night and seeing stars and a black sky, who cares?

As-long-as they're not sleeping on a hard ground and in some cases, in the cold, wishing they had a nice comfortable warm bed without worries, having food in their stomach and a nice hot shower, that's the most important thing for them.

Back during the medieval times in Europe, there were poor people called **"PAUPERS."** Paupers were people who roamed the streets, with nowhere to go, down on their luck with no money or cash flow coming into their pockets. Forced to beg, steal, and hustle in order to survive. These types of people were forced to receive help from their rulers or government during that time period, and needed a roof over their heads. The type of shelter that was provided for Paupers was called, an "ALMSHOUSE." An Almshouse goes back to the 10th Century. The first recorded institution was in York, by King Athelstan, going back to the middle ages circa 1132. Almshouses were built for people who weren't in the position to care for themselves or their families. It was also for the mentally ill, old, children, and criminals, all fused into one.

During that time those types of institutions were started and run by charities, religious groups, the people and government. It was during the Queen Elizabeth era when she came out with the poor laws, which stated that the poor should be tended to and taken care of. Material things should be provided for them to help with their survival. Buildings should be built; they should be clothed, fed, etc.

The Almshouses were shelters, slash jails, slash mental institutions, slash hospitals, slash elderly homes and slash juvenile facilities all in one . . . crazy right?

If an individual was sentenced by the courts, they would find themselves going to an Almshouse to live out their sentence. There were staff members there to deal with your individual situation. Almshouses during that time were not the greatest places to live. For one, the food was terrible; it was stuffy, cramped, overcrowded and diseased. They would divide the Paupers and inmates into groups. The women had their sections and rooms, or floors. The men and children had their separate sections as well. Depending on your situation there was a section for you.

If a child was too young (two years old and younger) they would have to stay with their mother until they were older, if she was still there. The rules and regulations [on America soil] changed as the decades passed. For instance:

Children were no longer permitted to live and work amongst the adults (they went into orphanages.) The individuals who ran these harsh institutions were called overseers.

In England, once a Pauper committed himself to living in an Almshouse, they were at the mercy of the institution. They had to work extremely hard. The male Paupers and the inmates worked in the fields, by breaking and smashing boulders and picking oakum, or crushing bones, etc.

The women and girls worked in sewing shops. They washed and cleaned, as-well-as babysat the younger ones.

As time went on in these same institutions in early America, the kids did not go to school, they worked. But as time progressed, they found it wise for the kids to go to school, so they could have a positive effect on the future of the country, in the new world. The mind set was, if the children went to school (on the premises and off) they would have less of a chance of reentering these Almshouses again, and following in the footsteps of their parents.

Many immigrants had come to America from England and other parts of Europe as indentured servants (including the kids) to make a better life for themselves. The European system in the Almshouse was to separate those who acted out and had trouble with the law, and try to convert them into good law abiding citizens.

In the early 1900's in America, there were many changes within the system with the Almshouse slowly converting into what they called` *"the Poorhouse,"* which again derived from England.

Now once you enter the Poorhouse (with your family, if any) you were strictly at the mercy of the institution. They could do as they pleased with you and your family.

You gave up all your rights as an individual and handed it to the [county] government.

While residing there, you had to wear certain kinds of clothing that was provided to you and your family by the person in charge, which was the overseer or master.

Unlike the Almshouse, the Poor house was more organized; there were doctors, nurses, and teachers. Punishment was harsh for misbehavior. Paupers were beaten and then confined to their rooms or cells.

Now, the old and sick in many cases were not capable of doing the type of work that needed to be done within these asylums. These types of people were called "Enabled bodies." The people who had the strength and were capable of hard work were called "Abled bodies." The old and sick most likely spend the rest of their days being cared for by the government, or charity. Chances are they would die living in these institutions, and buried on the institutional grounds. The county would put you (and the children) in a wooden box, place you in the burial area, and think no more about you; with no tombstone or anything to identify you. There were not many records kept in the process, because to them you were nothing.

Some of the overseers or masters in charge of the process were very crooked people. They would rape the women and children (children were found missing in some institutions) and take the money that was for the food and clothing.

Most of these women were left alone with no man or husband (in many cases he died and left his family with no money or valuables.) So, she was forced to go into the system for support, like the present. The institution was deliberately run in a foul manner to discourage the people from entering, in hope that they would find a way to fend for themselves. If a woman got pregnant while in the system she was responsible for the care of the baby, not the man (married or not.)

Two famous individuals lived in theses nasty asylums, a man by the name of Charlie Chaplain and a woman by the name of Ann Sullivan (who cared for a blind and deaf young lady by the name of Helen Keller.) Some houses were run by Christians; others were run by Protestants, etc. They may have been English, French, Irish and the likes. Everyone wanted to stay within their own religion and culture. Around this time there was a lot of industrialization going on, which lead to a boom in urbanization and more immigration.

America again had advanced to a new type of insti-tution in the countryside called, "**The Poor farm**." This asylum was not much different from the Poorhouse.

Here the inmates and Paupers worked on a farm where there where vegetables, hogs, beef, chickens and other animals to deal with. Again, they were all divided up according to their issues. The inmates there sentenced by the courts worked in crews on the roads. Working on these

Poor farms put food in ones stomach. They did not work and sell what they produced, it was for them.

Each Poor farm was different (as all the other institutions.) Some Poor Farms had the Paupers pick cotton, which could be used for clothing. The buildings were built differently as well. Some of them were built erect (straight up) with more than one floor, and some had just one level, but long, they all varied to house the inmates and indigent people.

There were no more than 15 to 20 individuals living on these Poor farms. Some were known to have up to 30 indigents people. The format inside some of the institutions was large rooms everyone slept in, with lots of beds. Some institutions were over populated, with a kitchen, bathroom and lounge area. In some cases these buildings were built out of brick or concrete. Every county was responsible for the caring of their poor in the community. In some cases the government did nothing to help, the poor relied on the people or churches.

The overseers (or masters) did a lot of work in these establishments, as-well-as off grounds pertaining to the shelter. They made sure that everything was going accordingly. Their pay was about $300 yearly. The master hires and fires guards, laborers and managers.

In certain asylums the security is in the front as you enter the building. There's only one way out and no fire codes. If you were a mother and you decided to leave, you must take your little one(s) with you, as they do in shelters now.

Mothers then have been known to step out and leave their little ones never to come back (sad I know.)

Now, these types of shelters began to fade away in the mid 1900's, about the time the Social Security act came about in 1935; finances to aid mothers (the dates in the history of these events are not clear in a lot of instances, remember, a lot of records were not kept, or, kept poorly, so each historian or author may have a different date concerning that time.)

In those days, institutions were in great need of everything; otherwise you would have homeless people everywhere and out of control crime.

Some of these places were clean, some were filthy with roaches, flies and rodents (remember as I stated in my last book, every shelter is different, like every state is run differently, the same applies to back then.) Some of the asylums had good decent people who cared for the unfortunate, and a lot didn't.

These modern day shelters were for the unfortunate. To house them, give them work and a fighting chance to get back on their feet and rebuild their lives. As time when on, ways changed, there was slow improvement, but improvement happened.

With children being abused living there, and robbery taking place, new laws came about in order to improve care, as-well-as the direction of America.

In time, more programs were added into the equation because of unfortunate incidents and the increase in homeless people. More respect for mothers with children emerged; more help going out to families blossomed in order to keep them together and off the streets and out of poor institutions.

The government attempted to keep mothers with their children, who may have abandoned them because of the stress of caring for the family without the help of the father, or government at that particular time, as-well-as being jobless.

Note: Our shelters are here today because of the institutions of yesteryear, which is a tremendous improvement since the 17, 18, and 1900's. The psychological part of living in a shelter is tough, dealing with the rules and regulations of the system, the overcrowded conditions and the disrespect from everyone, including the workers. The stress and depression that the women back then and now go through. The shame, and the tears, of being in a place like that for the sake of the children, which can also have an impact on their schooling . . . its mind boggling.

All said goes towards the mentality which still exists today, just in a different way, because of the difference in times.

Men must care for the children they help bring into this divided, unjust, greedy, racist world. They must have more financial input on helping the mother. This will take pressure off the mother, and keep families out of the shelters, then and now. Men back then got women pregnant, and left them to care for the children alone, just to move on and get another woman pregnant . . . disgusting!

Yes, yes, yes, of course there will still be homelessness, but not on the level it is today if we men took on our part. Men play a major role in homelessness; if the economy is thriving they should be working, providing, with no damn excuses! If not, they should still be a part of their children's lives no matter what the situation.

If a woman finds herself in the system and there's no child involved, then that's on her (which there may be other reasons behind that.)A shelter is no place for a child, especially while in school; it interferes with the child's learning and self-esteem. Other kids will tease him/her which can interfere with them going to the next grade, keep that in mind, if you are living in the shelter system anywhere in the world.

Chapter 2

Keepin My Sanity

First of all I want to praise the highest above and that's god. It's important that one put him first. If you put him first, he will put you first . . . and deliver. But you must talk to him, and make an effort to pursue what it is you are praying for.

I will mention our father and Jesus often while you read this informative elevating book.

Now after spending two and a half years in the New York City shelter system and dealing with the misery and negativity that comes along with living there, I was forced to continue in spite of my stress level, and to a lower degree depression. Depressed because I didn't get in and out as I thought I would. Also because of the fact that my boys had to endure the bull that goes on within the system, as I was constantly working, and running around trying to make life easy for them and more.

I would sit up late at night when I would put them to bed, and contemplate, and take in what was going on in our lives. My mind was foggy. I could not think straight due to so many things going on in my brain at once. I used sex to relax me, and put me to sleep. If you didn't know, good sex and sleep together helps heal the mental and the physical, at least for me. My body at that time needed it.

Once I got enough sleep after engaging in such an act, my body felt much better. Not 100% . . . in order for me to feel like that, I needed to be out of that environment, altogether! Nonetheless I felt better than before, or that prior day. Why, because the center of my body was tense like one big ball of stress built up in my chest, "literally." It came from the accumulation of different emotions and issues.

After, I no longer felt out of touch with the natural forces around me, which is the movement of the earth and the heavenly bodies. I felt at ease on the inside, in sync with the universe. My mind after this great rest was no longer mixed up with important and unimportant thoughts popping up uncontrollably.

-I was at ease-

Now once I was up, I was able to sort out my thoughts and put things in perspective. I was able to move forward with want I needed to do. I want you to know that raising three babies without a spouse or mate (outside of other problems) will take its toll on you. I am a good loving father who cares for his kids **"deeply!"** But running around daily, taking care of the needs babies demand and command will bug you out and have you screaming for relief and time for yourself.

I was so over the edge, I sat up in my shelter apartment and cried; it was unbearable. I often contemplated leaving, but hung in there, for the sake of my sons. Again and again I would talk to Jehovah. I choked it up, put my son's needs in front of mine and told myself constantly . . . I will be out of here in due time.

It was my first year in the shelter with more months and stress to come. I kept cool and strong. I had the forces above with me and used certain techniques to get me by, in order to contain my emotions and stay calm.

In due time (with praying of course) I made it through my first and second year. Struggling while in the last couple of months, I was to a point where I was ready to destroy anyone who messed with any of my sons (they do that in the shelter . . . bullies.) I would argue, and let off some steam (you can't keep holding things in, you must let it out) every now and then . . . even fight. That was a must at times, or you would be picked on. That happened mostly in the first shelter and the first year.

As time progressed, I would learn how to deal with certain individuals around me who caused me pain. I began to learn how to deal with the daily hostile environment. And the stress from dealing with my job, and the fact that I had to look for an apartment, etc. (I maintain myself.)

I began to get better at handling the rude behavior from the Leaches and the Loungers (to understand these terms, buy the book "Sheltered.") I began to learn more on how to deal with people who basically had no lives, and needed to bring you down to their level in order for them to feel good about themselves. As I got closer and closer to leaving the system, my coping skills and patients got improved considerably. I began to take my newly discovered "know how" and applied it to other areas of my life (like my job for instance.)

I began to have more control of what was happening around me, and what I did and didn't allow it to affect me.

It's like learning new motor skills as a baby. I then used those skills to help me to weather and control my insides, which will hopefully help me to live longer in the long run (with God's blessings of course.) Like a baby's newly discovered motor skills. I began to learn how to control it and use it when needed. I practiced more by applying those skills to different situations and issues in my life.

I was now certified to begin to look for an apartment, and was constantly let down by owners and supers, telling me that apartments were not available . . . and they were. Or, real-estate agents telling me they had nothing for me to see at the time. It was frustrating, very frustrating, especially after days and months of searching.

I would suck it all in, rest for a couple of days build up my tolerance level and will power and rid myself of my frustrations. Think positive, and of course talk to the man above. I would ask him to give me the strength to endure the negativity and racism people had towards me and my sons, as I tried to rent an apartment in their neighborhood.

I endured the foul mentality they displayed towards me, prayed for them, and went back out to search for a home for my babies . . . believing and knowing that in time I would have an apartment . . . soon, by staying positive and providing effort, in spite of the devil trying to bring me down. Thank God I later found a place in the Bronx.

Chapter 3

The Boogie Down

Leaving the shelter is one of the greatest feelings I ever felt in my life, I was overwhelmed with happiness. In time I drove my car (I had got) everywhere in Queens looking for an apartment under Section 8, but could not find anything. I was told Section 8 in Queens was scarce. After looking but for so long, I decided to begin looking in the Bronx. If I didn't have my boys I would have hung in there looking in Queens. But my sons needed to get out of that environment as-soon-as possible, so I decided to look in the Bronx.

Finally, I found something suitable for my boys and me, near the Bronx criminal court, on 161street. I wasn't feeling it but I needed out of that shelter system . . . Now! It had a nice big living room and two decent sized bedrooms.

In time I began to meet people in the area. Across the street from me was a small park with a playground. I took my sons their often to relax. I admitted them into school and began to search for a baby sitter, which was a task, because I knew no one. I got lucky, because the lady upstairs gave me a hand. I wasn't feeling her man much, but, I needed help.

As time passed I met a young lady by the name of Kiki. She had problems in the last apartment she was living in and decided to live with me for a spell. She did a lot for me; she babysat the boys while I took care of life's importance.

She cleaned the house, cooked the food, and of course took care of my needs. But there was a problem I didn't see at all . . . she was a crack head. Something I never encountered in a relationship with a woman before. I noticed that money began to be missing at various times. I would count my money and be short. I then began to give her stares with silence.

When I questioned her concerning the matter she would look at me as though I was crazy and deny any wrong doing, which I expected. After a while I knew I could not trust her. She was a liar as I knew addicts were. I found out she was on crack when one of her so called friends spilled the beans on her. I was in awe; I always wondered why she had white build up around the corner of her mouth.

Her friends told me that it was her thirst for a hit. I've been in the streets and have a bit of street knowledge and never knew that. Kiki would be quiet at times, and if I would engage her in conversation about something she would have an attitude, as-well-as headaches (crack head symptoms.)

In time I would discover more serious unseen flaws about her, and let her go. I worked, paid bills, brought food and also gave her money, and here she is stabbing me in the back. No booboo . . . I don't think so, "see ya," you're out of here. No matter who was in my life at the time I was the one holding things down, and cared for my sons. I don't want anyone coming into my life and having more of an impact on my sons than me, no one. At this point in time, not even their mother.

If I don't have a woman in my life to help me, I won't be as patient with my boys. Because a woman keeps me grounded, they keep me in check when I go overboard with my sons, as-far-as disciplining is concerned.

I love my sons, but would come home from work at times and not be in a good mood. I would pick my boys up from their babysitter's house, bring them home and instantly start getting ready for the next day.

I ironed their clothes, helped them with their homework, all the while food is cooking in the oven or on the stove. I would give them a shower and then eat. I'd then sit while they were in bed (often) and talk with them about life and see how their day was, and see what was on their little minds.

Going food shopping and clothes shopping was too much for me, because that crap was not in my nature to do. Walking around, trying to find the correct size that fits, no, no, no. Jumping from store to store, oh no. It was tiresome and frustrating for me. That's something that women do and have the patients for, much more than men. There were times I felt over whelmed and out of place caring for my little boys. That's why I get on men about being there for their children, because women have been doing these kinds of chores forever. I wasn't the patient type, I had to learn, as-well-as coping skills throughout my experiences raising my boys, and dealing with life.

I would ask God for help and assistance raising them. I was more patient in dealing with nasty mouthed women as opposed to handling my boys' energy, aggression and needs. It was extremely difficult for me at that time, but I stayed positive, looked inside of me and allowed the love I have for them to hold me up and lead the way. I knew that with me in their lives what affect that could have. That kept me strong and focused on a daily basis.

Anyway, I managed, with little help from no one after a while. I did receive opinions on how to raise and handle them. I could have kept the individuals opinion or dump it, it was my choice. In time I had other women come in and out our lives who had children and had some kind of an effect on me raising my boys, because women in most cases are natural nurses and care takers when it comes to direct care.

I embraced their gifts and tried to pick up on their points, like, being more affectionate towards the needs of a child (holding, foundling, pampering.) I believe there are times a person should be stern and times when one should be humble, and allow your guards to come down and allow others to affect your thought patterns. If you don't know something, and are true to yourself, and know when you need help and are wrong, let a person help you. I try to be careful and selective about allowing and not allowing influences to come into my world. But when it comes to kids you must try to be intelligent and fair for their sake, in order for them to be the best they can be as adults.

Well, in time I met this young lady by the name of Meka. I met her picking up my boys from school one day. She was about short and pretty. We went out a couple of times, I then met her family. She was adopted, and loved her family. Especially the way her adopted mother treated her (in a very loving manner.)

In time we would come together as a couple. She would stay over my house because she didn't feel at home staying with certain adopted family members, it was over crowed. She was about 25 years of age when I met her at the time. She didn't cook much and really didn't want to work. All she wanted to do was lay around eat and ride me when she had the chance. In time, I insisted she find a job if she wanted to live in my house. She didn't help me with the kids at the time because she didn't know much about raising kids.

Note: when you deal with anyone who comes into your life and they have to deal with their lover's children, there's a chance that person will have a problem with one of the children (the least.) The more kids there are the more of a chance there will be friction in the family and with the new mate.

Well, Meka had a problem with my middle son at the time. When you have problems of that magnitude, the children's parent will be in the middle of everything. There will be even more of a problem if the blood child is a teenager. She was a Gemini and he is a Scorpio (ya feel me.) I taught him to respect his Elders; he was about 9 years old at the time. He was very out spoken and voiced his opinion; I wanted him to be himself with respect.

But she herself had a fresh mouth and could fib her tail off, but had her good points as well.

She would help me with my boys as-far-as bringing us together as family was concerned. She would tell me I needed to do more things as a family like: go to the park, have family meetings (which I already was into) to see what was on the minds of my boys, as I did what she suggested and more. During Christmas she made a big difference, because she brought stockings that had cartoon characters on them, and put small gifts in them, and made the Christmas tree look appealing the way she stacked presents around it.

She made the holiday season feel like a holiday. She brought a sense of calm to the house hold and took a lot of stress off of my back.

My boys would run to her for a female's perspective, as-well-as T.L.C. She cooked when she felt like it, and cleaned the house, and in time paid bills. It helped me deal with life a little better. Having her there brought a degree of relaxation and peace to the house. But I also had to deal with her baby side, her whining, her laziness, and lying ways. That made me upset because I felt like I had another child to contend with to an extent.

But, I liked her and was considering marring her. But I had to get to know her and see if I could deal with her ways. Of course I'm not a saint. I have my ways she had to deal with as well, which I had to change if we were to be one. She too wanted to marry me; she loved me as she said. I had deep feelings for her, but she was immature and needed to grow mentally. Nonetheless I stayed with her to see if she would change as I attempted to do.

She complained that I didn't give her enough attention (I didn't think that to be true but I made an attempt to do something about it.) Everyone around me knows that I love having my woman with me where I go. She also said that I didn't engage in conversation with her. It wasn't the age gap with her; it was her inexperience in life that stymied that and her laid back disposition.

She only talked about her job (when she got one.) That was it, nothing else. She didn't talk about sports, politics, or history, nothing interesting. We would have literally a five minute conversation on the phone and a little more in person. There was always a long pause with her.

Regardless of how I felt about her, I would still listen and give advice for her state of mind, for the sake of the relationship. All-in-all she was my woman and a part of my life, I wanted things to work. I was less likely to physically discipline my sons if they did something to really upset me when I had a caring woman in my life. Because women got on me when they thought I was wrong, I needed that and embraced it.

Chapter 4

One big stress ball

In about two years of living in the Bronx, I had a lot of battles, mostly due to my son being picked on. If you're in a situation and predicament where you are overwhelmed, and it seems that everything is against you. Do not hesitate to talk to God, very little can go your way, or you can go but so far if he is not in your life. Yes you can get far with the devil in your corner, but you will not stay there; your world will eventually come tumbling down.

Look at these drug kingpins, and dictators who want to rule the world, they don't last. You must have God in your life and must be doing the right thing, if you want peace and to make progress . . . and stay there, "Praise the lord!"

Near the court house of the Bronx, there were rude and negative people in the area. For instance: I had a neighbor on the second floor who just moved in, who had this male friend of hers who used to beat on her . . . often! The police would come to her apartment because she'd call due to him abusing her. But all that was for nothing, because she would allow him back in the house again.

In the beginning I had no problem with her man. We would talk [a little] and say hi and bye, that's how I kept it, until life says it should progress. Anyway, one night he was kicking her butt, and I could hear them down in my apartment (Her bedroom was right above mine.) I heard yelling and screaming. I wanted to tell them to keep the noise down my sons had school in the morning, and if anything interferes with their schooling, I have a lot to say.

However, in this case I let it go, just to avoid trouble. When you have a family and have an ego, you must bite it for the sake of the family. So the fight wound up coming down stairs to my floor (ground floor.) Now I could really hear everything.

She told him to leave and of course he didn't. All of a sudden I heard her gasping for air, as he grabbed her by the neck. I tried to block them out and mind my business but I couldn't.

He then took her head and smashed it into the sheet rock wall (she later told me) that was on the side where my room was, near the entrance to my apartment. When I came out the apartment the next day to go to work, I saw bits and pieces of sheet rock on the floor near the entrance to my apartment, and a big hole in the wall. There were also screws on the floor as well.

Now I'm upset because my boys play in the hall at times, or, just walking to go outside, or even coming in. They could step on one of those screws, or trip and fall because of the mess.

So, I decided to knock on her door and tell her about my concerns. She said that she would get it up, so I left it as is. One day passed, three days passed, a week passed. I finally saw her man and told him about it (hey, I shouldn't have to do it, they should respect their neighbors), he also said it will be removed and nothing happened.

About two weeks passed and I'm still walking around this trash, and the owner hasn't come around. I saw the abuser again and he had just gotten out of another argument with her. My timing was bad, I asked him about the pile they never got up. So I guess he wasn't feeling me at the time. He began cussing and yelling saying he isn't doing nothing and jumped in my face and pushed me. Ha-ha, I wasn't having that . . .

And it was on!!!

I began to jab at him and followed that up with right fist punches. After a couple of those, that was too much for his short thick body, so he grabbed me by the legs and got me on the floor. We began to grapple with extreme energy. One of my exes (live in) just so happened to be at the door way worried like hell. Within a couple of minutes the abuser somehow got me in a hold where I could not escape from. He grabbed me by the neck and his strong short legs were clamped around my legs.

He began to apply pressure to my neck area, I couldn't move. I began to gasp for air and was about to black out.

I had to get out of that hold and quick (I began to brain storm), as I was gasping for air and hearing my lady scream my name, I made moves to escape his death grip. I tried to grab his eyes but he kept moving his head . . . time for me was running out. There was one more thing I could do and it was in my face . . . "His Balls" (hey, all is fair in war), I grabbed them with force.
Guess what?
Bingo!!!
I was free, Ha-Ha!

Still gasping for air and somewhat dizzy, I got to my feet as we began to box again. Both of us tired as hell, exhausted from the ground battle. He was more tired than I was. So he tried to make a break for it and go out the front door, but I wasn't having it and continued to bring the noise, with a series of combos, but, as he, I was tired and allowed him to leave.

As he left I told him, we will go at it again if that garbage doesn't come up. I analyzed my actions after everything was over, and I could have handled that situation in another manner, a more mature way.

If he was a more dangerous thug I may have been seriously hurt or in the hospital. I could have even set my sons up for future problems.

Not good thinking on my behalf. I was thinking, I should have just picked up the pile of garbage myself instead of my ego dictating the actions.

May the lord help me with better judgment in the future. It shouldn't be about being a punk or soft.

There was another situation that involved my sons directly as I came home from work to pick them up one evening. This whole scenario blew me away, because my sons could have really been hurt.

One day I got home from work, put my bags down, had a little snack and proceeded to go to a nearby church and pick my boys up. Akeem and Alijah, they were about 6 and 7 years of age then.

I usually send them to a small church up the block after school where they were able to do their school work and get the word of God at the same time. They though it was boring. It was good for me as a way to get babysitting until I got home from work, and it was free. I attended this church at times as well, so they could learn more about the word.

Anyway, as I was coming up the hill I saw my eldest son Alijah running down the hill, doing 90 miles an hour. I was in the middle of the street crossing over at the time. Going on the side they were on.
Now I'm thinking what the . . . ?
And where's Akeem?!

As I looked further up the block he was right behind his brother some yards away, also running but not nearly as fast, doing 60.

Again, I'm thinking what the? As my confused mind continued to analyze the scene, which up to now was totally unpleasant.

I looked right behind Akeem (who just so happened to trip and fall) and there was a group of boys about their age and a little older, running them down.

There must have been about five of them. Alijah was running so fast he ran right by me (although I was still crossing the street.) When my son Akeem fell and I saw the reason why, I instantly stopped the delinquents in their tracks. Lucky for me and my sons I was coming because they would not have been nice to him while on the ground (thank you Jesus.)

When the boys saw me as I gave them a disturbing stare, they looked at me and then at my sons, like they had to get to them. I helped my son to his feet, and said to the tyrants in a stern puzzled voice, what the hell are ya'll doing.

The littlest one about Akeems size but shorter, stood his ground as the others slowly retreated, and said to my boys, "We'll get you tomorrow." As I called him to come closer he gave me negative feedback with a nasty look on his face.

After that incident, I wanted out of the Bronx, especially that area, because now I had to worry about the safety of my sons when I wasn't around, even more. If you are an involved loving parent, you know just what I'm talking about. I would get in touch with the church and tell them what was going on with my sons. They said they would keep my boys there after dismissal, until I got there, and believe you me after work I made no stops, straight to the Bronx to get my sons.

I would pray at night and ask God to be with me while we were apart. The best thing for me was to get from that area . . . period, and possibly the Bronx altogether. If I could, I would meet with the parents of all the boys, and let them know after that incident, if their child so much as looks at any of my boys wrong I will have them arrested.

With so many black boys not graduating and in jail I would not want that, but if the parents are not doing their jobs by instilling love and respect in the hearts of our ailing youngsters, I will have to do what I must do, because this is the safety of my boys, which comes first.

You don't have to be a parent in order to understand that. One of the reasons why I was so anxious to leave the Bronx with my boys is because of other incidents not concerning me that were going on while I was residing near the 161st Street and Webster Avenue area.

Post shelter life, I experienced an abundance of angry, selfish people who wanted to bring you down to their unhappy mental level. And will do whatever they can to make that a reality. And you as a clear level headed, giving, loving, individual by all means cannot allow that to transpire.

The devil is everywhere and to a degree in all of us. This is why, you, me, we, must have Jesus Christ in our minds heart and souls, because the devil doesn't want a little of you, he doesn't just want you to think of negativity, he wants you to act it out, and consume you with hate and violence. We all think of negative things in our minds, some people more than others. It's when we act it out more-and-more and not accept Jesus in our hearts, to counter the devilish thoughts turned into actions, is when it becomes a big problem.

One must ask God to forgive your devilish thoughts, and rebuke satan, in the name of Jesus. Lord God knows we are not perfect; this is why we must believe in him and try your best to walk a straight line of righteousness as-much-as possible.

Anyway, living in that part of the Bronx (because there are some good parts of the Bronx that has less crime in the neighborhood) where there are people who like anarchy and trouble was not cool. Some people enjoy living their lives around constant negativity and trouble, not me.

Now, around my second year living in that area there was this guy I met. He was southern and had a wife from New York (Decent man.) They had a son that was about 11 and a daughter about 13. His woman was one of those ghetto types that ran her mouth and felt she should be in control, and had no job. He was working, but his wife was boss.

Anyway, I told you about the park across the street from me. I would see her there with her kids.

To make a long story short, the mother and I didn't get along, because she tried talking to me with her ghetto manner, and I wasn't going for it. I would let her know that I'm not your husband or kids, and she was not going to talk to me in the manner that she was accustomed to. She wasn't feeling that, so that was the beginning of us not getting along.

I would converse with her husband, but when she came in our presence, I would be a mute towards her. So one day our kids got into a problem in the park. Her daughter who was similar to her mother and my son Alijah got into a little problem. She wasn't feeling what I had to say about the kids little disagreement, which I let the mother know what, was and wasn't happening.

So she made a scene, which was to be expected. One thing led to another, and the next thing I know she was threatening me. She said that she was going to get someone to kick my ass (being that she couldn't do it.)

So days went by . . . nothing! Not thinking much about it anymore, I was coming out of my house with my boys and saw her and she began going off with the mouth, in no time about four young black males was up in my face . . . BLOODS!

There was a short kid and a tall one about 6' 2" and stocky. The other two were average size. So, in my experience the short ones always had something to say; he asked me was I messing with his aunt (your aunt yeah sure, I'm thinking.) And I told him it was the other way around, like he cared. Meanwhile she was standing there sipping on her drink with a smile on her face, as the short one decided to jump further in my face, as his boys began to surround me. I began to take steps backwards. At this time I heard the ghetto woman saying "I don't hear you running your mouth now."

All of a sudden the big kid swung on me. He balled up his fist and cocked his arm back (which I saw coming a mile away) like he was a top winding himself up to be spun. I ducked as I continued to back away, trying to be humble and not get hit, at the same time watching out for my sons. My boys began to cry, as my middle son Akeem made an attempt to help his dad. But an adult held them back to keep them out of harm's way.

As I was still back peddling the short one ran up on me and punched me in the jaw (it was weak), he's lucky he had his goons with him, otherwise he would have gotten his butt whipped by Mr. Parks. I had to think about my sons at the time, taking a glance over at them just about every ten seconds to make sure they were ok.

My safety and health was important so I did nothing to retaliate. And they took full advantage of that. Finally a lady from a house across the street yelled out of her window, "I called the police, their coming" thank God I though, that could have been serious, as they retreated.

I didn't want my boys to see their father get a beat down. That would not have been good for their little minds. Now, when I would see the ghetto woman in the streets I would not say a word to her at all, and she did the same. I wanted to call the police on her, but it would have only caused more future problems, and with my sons with me constantly that would not have been any good.

I didn't need any more surprises; the results may have been a lot different, so I completely let it go and left it to God. At this time I just said hi and buy to the husband. He was there all the while and could have told his boss to drop everything, especially being that I had my sons. But he didn't. I stayed positive while living on the same block as them, watching my back (I hate doing that.) I sat my boys down after the event (once home) and told them the lady wasn't a nice person, and God will take care of her in due time.

I was ok, no bruises no scares, I had a smile on my face so they would be at ease. They really wanted to know why someone would hurt their dear old lovable dad. As I explained to them there are bad people in this world, and we must stay away from them. I answered their questions to keep them at ease, and at the end of it all which was about 20-30 minutes, I gave them a big hug, which was reassuring to them and a big kiss. I used to kiss my boys on the lips back then; that's how much I love them.

Chapter 5

If you believe

My two year lease was about to expire and being that I didn't get along with the land lords wife, I decided to leave. I decided to leave the Bronx and go to Queens to find an apartment.

Once I got to Queens I had a female real estate agent help me to search the area. Her son who worked with her found me a three bedroom apartment. The landlord who was an old, in good shape (about 75 years old) Jamaican lady, decided to take my Sec.8.

I told Sec.8 about the apartment and they came down to inspect it for the first time, and it failed, because there was a bubble in the bathroom tile ceiling, that used to leak.

It dropped about four inches down, like it was pregnant. It had a stain in it that looked like piss, and looked as though it was about to burst. So in order for me to move in, the ceiling had to be fixed. I never fixed a ceiling in my life and didn't know where to start. But my time in the Bronx apartment was up and the landlord and her husband had plans for it. I had to leave . . . soon!

So that bathroom ceiling had to be fixed. I decided to use the brains that God gave me and do it myself. The ceiling must have been about five yards long and four feet across. I had to remove about three yards long of it, and two and a half feet across. It was at least three inches thick because the tiles were doubled. In order for me to move in, it must be done, and now. The land lord wasn't paying for anyone to come fix it. So I took my money and bought what was necessary for it to be fixed.

I started as-soon-as I could, and would have the land lord take it out of my rent payment (I know ya'll didn't think I was going to give her my services and money for free now did ya . . . not!)

I would come from the Bronx to Queens daily to fix it. I had to remove the bad area of the ceiling out after I measured everything for the new sheet rock that was to be put up. I had to cut this and pull out that which was no good. Hammer this, screw that, ha-ha I made a big mess.

Within a couple of days I was done. It looked wonderful. I was impressed with the job; the landlord was impressed as well. I was very proud of the work I did. I was determined to get the apartment and I did what I needed to do in order to get me and my boys in there.

I put my mind to something that I needed and wanted. When I finished the painting, it was like a professional did it.

It comes to show that if an individual wants and needs something, there's nothing that can stop the person, and in this case it was an accomplishment for me. I looked at how I disassembled it and brought the same materials needed in order to put it back together as was. I was determined to fulfill my goals and desires. Well, in the long run, the apartment was approved and I was in. I brought my shorty with me at the time (my woman), her name was Meka.

I told her if she comes to stay with me she would have to get a job, and help me with some of the bills. No freebees BooBoo, and in time she did just that, with me pushing her on. She got a job working with the mentally ill. She paid for the gas, electric and food, I paid the rent, "strictly."

In time we would do things as a family. We'd go to the park, go jogging, and play basketball; she was good for the family. I would take my sons to the park without her, and teach them how to play different sports and let them learn to get into the habit of exercising.

One year my little lady gave me a surprise birthday party, just me her and the kids, there was cake, ice cream, and they sung happy birthday, it was really nice. My sons liked her, they had an off and on relationship. When we would go dancing she would never like to dance, and had no problem with me dancing with others. I personally want and love to dance with my lady, nonetheless we would still have fun. She would come up to the school whenever I would go, for whatever reason pertaining to the boys.

I was (am) hard on my boys when it comes to school. Having a good education is paramount for me, when it comes to any child; they are the future. Without them there is no sound future for the world. I try to instill independence in my sons.

I believe African-American parents should be hard on our kids, particularly in these days (were not doing a good job, as a community, at all.)

I tell them that they are number one and must take care of themselves as an individual and as brothers. There are two things that I don't go for pertaining to my sons, and that is fighting each other and not performing in school the way they are capable of. Those are felonies in my house which is approached with stiff penalties that they will not like. I love my boys and like any caring parent, want the best for them, they are good boys.

Well in due time my shorty and I would part. Unfortunately she wound up being a negative person untrue to herself, like so many other young ones were.

After about five years, it had to end. We didn't have much in common. Not because of the age gap (even though that played a slight role.) She didn't have enough experience in life which limited our conversation; she had a younger mind set, but very bright.

Often you have young women who want older men in order to fill in that father figure role they never had as a young girl. It could also be for a sexual reason, conversation wise, a financial reason (sugar daddy.)

Anyway, I had and have my faults in relationships and I'm steady trying to improve (for myself and for God) so when marriage comes around I'm a better more understanding person. I don't want my relationships to be based on sex alone I want a balance.

Well, when she left I was alone for a while, me and my boys. When I'm alone with them, particularly at night, I engage in long conversations about life, as-often-as I can, it's a bonding process, and I love it.

I would tell them what happened and why it happened, if I have knowledge of the topic (whatever topic.) I tell them how they can avoid having themselves in a bad situation.

I tell them what to do and how to do it. Accept the facts of the present situation if necessary, and strive to make the best out of that bad situation . . . and to stay positive.

You, me . . . we all, must push forward to turn a bad situation into a positive one. They sit and listen, and at times (not all ways) I will dish out constructive criticism . . . .
CONSTRUCTIVE!!!

I urge, ask, and often demand better, filled with love and sensitivity, and they can hear it in my voice. You must be careful while doing it; it can mess with their self-esteem. I like to give them food for thought. I try to get them to think before they do things. And let them know that America and their way of thinking and culture are not very nice to black men, if they would mess with Obama, the President of the United States, in a racist fashion . . . . who do you think you are?

I let them know how they need to prepare themselves for the future in this country. People say that when they see me with my boys, they feel I'm a good daddy, ha-ha (softly.) Actually, I have a lot more learning to do, because I can be too hard at times and too demanding.

No, I'm not perfect but I'm striving to be better than I am with my boys. Knowing in the future that they will understand why their daddy was so lovingly pushy.

I lived in a nice, kind of quiet area of Queens, off Liberty Avenue.

I lived on the door on my right side (from the outside.)

My neighbors on my left, would help me with my boys when needed, God bless them. My landlord who looked wonderful, talked about the lord . . . talked.

One day she threw my shorty's dog out in the street, that she allowed us to have in her house.
Check this out ladies . . .

"It was a puppy."

Because of a disagreement we had, not pertaining to the dog, no lie. The puppy went walking in the middle of street after a smell here and a smell there and a leak. Yep, not knowing the danger of cars. It was her house I couldn't do nothing.

Then as the dog was trotting away, she got into a car and drove away still running her mouth.

I was saying to myself look at this crap. I ran and got the dog, and brought it back to the house. My Meka wasn't home, but she was bugging out when I told her the story.

I didn't have any respect for the landlord after pulling that stunt. I hid the dog. Thank God it didn't bark much at all. In time we got rid of it. The landlord lived in another state, but visited N.Y. often, to check on her house.

Well, after me and my little lady parted, I met this woman, by the name of Sharon. At this time in life I'm thinking about settling down and getting married, even more. I wanted to marry my little lady, but no go.

When I met Sharon, it was like I really want to do this. She was tall with heels. She was verbal, spoke her mind and was trying, trying, to run the relationship.

I was like, ummm, hell no BooBoo!

She was thick, with a big back side and had full lips, just the way I love my black women. We got along good in the beginning. But as she got use to me, she wanted to start telling a brother what to do, and nagging about trivial things. She had a problem with my two eldest boys from time-to-time, not too much. They were in their early teens at the time.

Every woman I had in my past, loved my youngest child Ahmaud.

He's cute and extremely quiet, low voice and shy, teachers felt this way as well.

Sharon was like the rest of the women of the past, nice to the boys, cooked for us, and gave her opinion about everything. Gave T.L.C., and got on me concerning the boys when necessary.

I met her family, and she mine. She too wanted to get married, calling me her husband.

I personally am not marrying a woman who thinks she is going to run the relationship, hell no, it just isn't happening.

We hung out together and went dancing. Every night about the same time her body would shut down. Meaning she had to get some sleep. Sometimes she would get up and go to work with very little sleep, I was amazed. And she functioned the whole day until her body told her it was time to rest again.

She had no kids of her own. She took on her sisters kids, and had them ever since they were babies as-well-as toddlers. She took on all seven of them. Not at the same time, but in groups.

I wanted to marry Sharon, but again she thought she was gonna run the relationship. She wasn't lazy like a lot of the other women in my life. She would take a house apart and clean it. I was very fond of her.

At the time, I was working and holding down an apartment, just looking to progress in life. I was doing what a man was supposed to do, and more. I wasn't sitting around complaining about life, and being jobless. That was/is not how I get down as a man in life. I'm a provider and a fighter, trying to make a difference in other people's lives, and a college student (unfortunately no degree though.) That being the case, a woman is supposed to work with a man who's doing these deeds so there can be even more progress, and vice versa.

Not going against him by wanting everything her/their way, her way, her way, there will be arguments in the relationship and it will not flourish with me.

Well, in time we parted, it only lasted 9 months, her loss. I left her at the end of 2008. When we see each other we talk, I have nothing against her. At first I did but time heals all wounds, I talk to God and ask him for the strength to forgive and not be bitter against anyone.

I kept things moving, dedicating my attention to my boys, trying to be the best dad I can be, trying in my powers to give them what they need. They are doing very well in school.

I've been working in a Hospital for the last 24 years plus, I have no male friends because I always have attractive women and don't want to go through the bull of someone looking at the other. If he would try and make a pass at my lady I would flip on him, and if she allowed it I would flip on her as well and go to a level of nastiness they would not like, so no male friends. Maybe in the future, but now I don't think so.

When I used to live with my mother in my *"hey days,"* and traveled alone, I had some male friends then going to clubs. But I was usually alone, so if I had to leave and they wanted to stay, I didn't have to get no negative feedback. I enjoyed traveling like that at times.

Anyway after time crawled by, I was driving down Liberty Avenue, and came across a young lady about 25 years old from caribbean named Esha. She was about 5'9", and living with her boyfriend. She said he was beating on her and being extremely bossy. He brought her here to live with him and his mother. She wasn't getting along with none of his family and wanted to get away. But she had no job, and no family (as-far-as she knew) living in New York.

She was confused about what to do; she didn't want to go back to the life she ran from, where she was living a hectic unemployed life, about to get into things that she would regret.

But she didn't want to stay where she was and deal with the bull her boyfriend and his family members put her through. She needed someone to-talk-to with a lot on her mind, desperate to let it out (cough, cough . . . enter Mr. Parks.) I listened to her and told her to try and make the most balanced and wise decision she could come to.

She would say that she missed her family back at home, but needed a change (little did she know she had family in New York, which I will get into later.)

We talked on the phone every day, got to know each other. But life living with her man's family was getting worse. She was getting more hurt and depressed. She was thinking about going into the shelter system to get away from her situation.

I said, "The shelter," "well hell, I know all about the shelter system girl, and you don't want to go there." So, being the gentleman that I am. I told her she could come and stay with me until she gets on her feet (I just got over a relationship with Sharon and didn't want to rush into another one people, so don't judge.) She was so happy and accepted the offer. I told her she had to get a job and could move in when she was ready. She called me the next day and let me know she had broken up with her man, and told him she was going into the shelter. When she finally got to my crib, I gave her a couple of draws and some space to put her stuff, which wasn't much. My boys were ok with it, because they knew that if daddy had a woman living with us, life would be easier for them.

Things clicked with her and the boys. She and I would sit in the room and watch movies; she played music, and was a new energized person.

We had fun together. She was a serious person and silly at the same time, she was a Taurus. You want to know what's funny. She was the same sign as Sharon, but younger and born the same darn day, check that out, and similar.

They both sucked their thumbs when tired or thinking, the same thumb the same way, with the same look in their eyes. But Sharon had more of an attitude. That could be because she's been through more of life's ups and downs.

Sharon was a former addict, yep! With more bull crap coming her way in life, Esha may be just like Sharon in time. Stress, depression, and trauma will change . . . you, me, anyone, if you go through enough. God bless her, let's hope that don't happen, we all want a healthy happy life.

Again, women help me with my relationship with my boys; I welcome their input tremendously. We began to have a positive bond together and go out and party, she's an aggressive dancer, no matter so am I. So one day she was talking with her mother on the phone. Her mother just found out that she had relatives in America in New York City, and guess what?

In the area, where we live . . . oh sugar!

About a mile from my house, double oh sugar!

So we went to see her new family members she never knew. She had an aunt who had a big house with kids her age. I was so happy for her. I was just getting into her as a person, but it was a temporary thing, it's all good. Jesus is walking with her!

Her aunt had extra rooms, so that made things easier for her. She was out of my house in about a week. We still were friends. She found a job. The combination of my job hours opposing hers, we were not able to see each other as much. Plus, I was trying to push my book **"Sheltered."**

My boys were disappointed, they liked her. My son Alijah was really into her. He's a flashy dresser and a handsome boy. He has a nice build and loves showing it off.

He's learning about life slowly, as teens must. My boys are not allowed to hang in the streets; I don't want them to have a street mentality. But I do want them to have some kind of street sense, so people won't get over on them so easily. When they pick a friend, I approve of it. If I don't like the friend, they are not to hang with them any more . . . period!

Anyway, my son Akeem had a friend whom we lived with for 6 months; Akeems a smart boy, but a bit of a follower. He did everything his friend did, even began to laugh like him. His friend was a good boy to an extent, he wanted to act hard but he wasn't. I knew if my son hung with him he would be locked up in time.

I confronted my son about hanging with this individual and I talked to his friend as well, and told him I don't want him with my son unless he does a 360 in attitude and action. I told his friends mother as well.

I told my son if I see them together, or even in the area his friend lives, I would embarrass him in front of everyone. I've done it before, and when I say I will do something they know I would follow it through.

Now to my knowledge, ever sense he's been around this person, he's been smoking weed and drinking (he was busted drinking in school once), as-well-as me catching him doing things he shouldn't be doing. I'm on to him and he knows it.

Now the baby, who is now 15, is still into cartoons. He's a laid back person, likes girls, but is not into them on a mental level as-far-as walking them home, or, trying to get a kiss.

All of the women I had in my life pampered him, pushed me out of the way and catered to his needs. My son's wanted/needed female presence so bad at times, they would jump on the woman's side and go against me. Which wasn't cool, and I would put a bug in their ears and let them know that the woman may not last. If we would break up tomorrow they would have to deal with me, letting them know, a woman would manipulate a situation and play them against me. I told them women come in and out of my life, but they will always be there.

They are women, and are needed in the house hold, which daddy understands, but they may disappear in the long run. My boys did what they were told because they saw what daddy was going through with the women, and learned that they do play head games (not all), and began to understand my concerns even more.

They learned to be loyal; I don't lie to them, never! You have to teach certain things to kids as-well-as them picking things up from the outside.

I demanded respect and let them know who ultimately is in their corner, regardless of what they may feel about others. They do what daddy tells them to do, because I feed them. But I want them to see the truth with their own eyes, instead of forcing them to see things my way.

In time they picked up on my teachings, embraced it, and fell right into their place.

Now, my boys know their role in life. If someone has a problem with me, they defend me and let the person who's against me know, that they are on the side of their dad (even their mother), because I am and was always there for them. As years go by they see who's who. You have to be patient with kids and they will see in time who's right and who's wrong, as they grow. That's one of the reasons why I never lie to my boys, because I don't want anything coming back on me in the future.

If you have a child that gives you a hard time, work with him (or them) and show him that you are going to give him tough love, which is what teens these days need. Let them know that if they are doing things they shouldn't be doing, it won't get them far in life. They will love and admire you at a young age, because they feel the love, although you're hard on them.

When a child is young and you're not there to discipline them and guide them or, you're there but do very little to nothing. That child may disrespect you for not being involved, and talk back to you as they get older, if they feel you cheated them in life. They measure your love through your actions or lack of (I'm not talking about verbal or physical abuse, that's on another level.)

Chapter 6

Put your mind to it

Well after Esha left, months went by and I met this woman on my job by the name of Mary. She was half southern and half Jamaican, from the islands. She was tall and thick, and crazy over Darnell. She had two sons, my two eldest son's ages, and was working as a nurse at my hospital for two weeks and then left.

In her new hospital she began to work late hours. She would text me about how much she thinks about me, and wrote me letters about how much she wanted to be with me for the rest of her life, and that I was her soul mate. When she started with the soul mate thing, I knew from there that the relationship wasn't going to last. She just met me a couple of days back, and was rushing things already.

That wasn't a good sign for me. But I continued with the potential relationship.

I had a "this may not work out" feeling, but gave her a try. She was talking love and marriage, within a week, word, no lie. I wanted to get married, but we had to get to know each other first, I knew she was desperate for love.

We started to hang out daily. I told her as I did with Sharon, that I wasn't interested in sex; I just wanted to get to know her. But she couldn't wait, in a couple of weeks; she just had to have me, although I was willing to wait more time than that.

She just left a relationship and was ready for me now. I wanted to see her "Aids test" as-well-as mine, but she didn't care, she wanted me as-soon-as possible.

I was looking for a long distance relationship and wanted to take my time. I wanted marriage and knew what it took to get there, and quickly jumping into bed wasn't the way in my experiences. It was all about what's in the head with me. Can we sit and talk about different things, and not argue over petty crap. Remember in the beginning it's always good.

She and I would take all our boys to church as a family (this is what she wanted.) I wanted the boys to bond first; she was in a hurry to come together as a family. But as I could see all along it wasn't going to work out.

Her boys were spoiled for one, and their fathers weren't fully in their lives (different fathers.) They were laid back kids and would not let their guards down. I would tell my boys to be respectful and kind to her boys. But as I could see and my boys would tell me, her sons weren't as friendly as mine. I know at the time their mother told them to loosen up, but because she's been put through situations with other men, they were reluctant to get close to anyone.

So I told my boys to keep trying. Her youngest boy opened up some, but the eldest one who was 16 at the time didn't. My sons would complain about him not opening up. The mother continued to talk with him, but he stayed in his shell, even after months of us being together. So I didn't bother my sons about it no more. I told them if they didn't want to come together . . . then screw it.

Her youngest was 13 at the time, and my middle son got along swell. It was the two eldest who were the quiet ones that we had a problem with, because her eldest son didn't cooperate. I knew even more our relationship would not last because of that situation. But I continued, because I was into their mother, hoping in time the kids would come together and the mother would change some of her ways.

Our sex was off the chart, it was wonderful, and wild. Our souls seemed as though they came together.

I would go to events in Harlem, Brooklyn, and other places to sell my books and shirts. As I was trying to get sales (with her sitting in my face), I would talk to other women (who were mostly the book buyers) and give them my pitch. I would be up close at times so they could hear what I had to say, plus it was a way I expressed myself to show my seriousness.

I would even go as-far-as to touch their arm, gently! Why did I do that? She accused me of wanting to get with the woman (or women) and have a family (family part just kidding.) I was like are you for real; I'm trying to get a sale. For heaven's sake, your right here, but talking to her is like talking to a wall, really. Her accusing me of nonsense brought about problems and arguments.

What really took our relationship over the edge was the time I drove her to Long Island to take a test so she could start her new nursing job.

When she finished the test and we were about to leave, a white lady who was so kind to us during our stay, began to say goodbye to us. Now check this crap out.

We all were standing in a triangle like format, my lady was on my left, and the white lady was in front of us. Now I knew my lady was jealous, but I didn't really know to what degree. I learned just how deeply insecure she was that day. Check this out!

The white lady reached her hand out towards me, at the same time her upper part of her body began to lean in towards me, so, I thought she was giving me a good by hug, nothing sexual, just a nice friendly hug. So I leaned in as well, she proceeded to stretch her head and neck towards my face while shaking hands with me at the same time. She then gave me a peck on the cheek and said good bye, it was completely totally innocent.

Minutes later we got into the car and she flipped. Telling me I wanted her and I should have just fucked her right there. I wanted to marry her, but after that I was convinced it wasn't going to happen. Again, I was fond of her and continued with the relationship, because the sex was sensational as-well-as other little things. I've been in enough relationships to know that she wasn't going to change, although throughout the relationship, I tried to break bad habits that she wasn't feeling. For instance: she wants her man to wear slippers in the house. I wasn't used to that but in order to shut her up, I did it.

I also tried to stop touching people when I tried to sell my books or engage in friendly conversation. It was hard because I was doing it for so long, and really had no complaints in the past from others.

But she wasn't trying to do nothing. She wanted me to do all the changing and the things I didn't like concerning her, she continued to do. With her everything was tit-for-tat (if you can do it, so can I, was her attitude, and most of her arguments were petty.) She was in deep, deep denial in life, and was a serious hypocrite, and contradicted herself as well.

She had the attitude that, she could do things and I couldn't. Like she would go out with her girlfriends (as she says), while I was home in my apartment with my sons. However, once I began to do it, she had a big problem with it. She would accuse me of cheating while out, crazy right? I would tell her she needed help. The longer I stayed with her the more I really meant what I said.

The first year in our relationship she had me playing guessing games with her. She was in control, for a while, just let me say that. She had me buggin, on a mental trip.

One day I was selling my Obama football jersey and books (yes Obama, you will love it readers) in Manhattan, at my job's union hall. They gave a yearly event and there were other vendors there as well. I could not concentrate because, she was out with her girlfriend, texting me and saying she's around a lot of guys, and they were trying to rap to her. And she may go to another party after that one with the guys they met. And she may not come home tonight, she may stay over her girlfriend's house, just to fuck with me and see if I loved her, or, see how much power she had over me, and at that time she had a lot.

I would text her and tell her to bring her ass home, etc. I couldn't sell a thing, at all, she had control of my mind (I hated it, and began to look for a way out from her mental hold I allowed her to have on me.)

I made little money. Throughout the night I would text her while neglecting my business. She played with my head like a cat plays with an injured mouse before eating it.

I was into her (understatement), and she wanted to be with me, but I knew I couldn't allow her to mess with my mind as time progressed. So I began to look for patterns in her actions to see what she was actually doing and not doing to get over on me. I believe she loved me, but, she needed to be in control in her relationships and I don't allow no woman, no woman to control my thinking and actions, especially the way she controlled mine (But don't get me wrong, I truly respect a woman's opinion.)

The second year came, and I was looking to let her ass go, but I didn't for a couple of reasons. Reason one: the way she messed with my head the way she did. I never had a woman manipulate me that way, I had to figure out her thinking so no other woman would do the same, and fast. It would be a defeat for me mentally.

In the past if a woman would try some mental game on me, I would put her in her place as a man should and let her ass go. There was something about her that I had to figure out before I went on with my life, I couldn't let her play with me as so and move on. I had to figure her out, put her in her place (as I did), and move on, so I wouldn't feel the defeat and be led astray in life. Reason two: I felt for her.

Late in the relationship (as the months started to go by) I began to really realize that she had issues. In time, as I got to know her more and began to pick up on her patterns, and hear what her back ground was like from her, and what other people told me. I would begin to see that she had serious issues, that she herself could not understand and, or, get rid of instantly.

I began to figure out, she couldn't figure herself out. Some of the things she did to me, she would do to others in her past. I knew then she could not control herself, which began to open the door for me to see other things, to assist me in my emancipation from this mental roller-coaster she had me on and just to let ya'll know . . . *"I hate roller coasters!"*

I was on to something now!

I would begin to see when she says she's going to do certain things, she wouldn't do them; she just wanted to control me, see the look on my face when I disagreed.

Then she would often say . . . there's no ring on my finger. And I would tell her, and there ain't going to be, not as-long-as you're playing theses sick head games that I'm now catching on to.

Don't get me wrong we had wonderful times together.

Mary and I would go out dancing and enjoy each other's company, immensely.

I'm a great dancer, which she picked up a lot of my skill and moves on the dance floor, and will not admit to it . . . that's cool.

When we danced we had the club we were at (all of them) checking us out, we were good together.

We would go walking in the park, which she loved to do with ponds in them. We would hold hands and walk around the whole park (daylight or dark) having conversation. She's a wonderful nurse, wonderful. She likes to do things as a family, as most women. We would take all the boys to the park to play, and go to the pool on hot muggy days. We took them all roller skating, as the boys learned how to skate, and had a wonderful time.

She met my family as-well-as me meeting hers. She called me daddy (a-ha-ha, hey!)

There were things that happen with the both of us, concerning family members, which weren't cool, but nothing major that involved the police or anything physical.

I don't have low self-esteem at all, I encourage women in my life to reach for the stars, no matter how I felt about them (I want the best for all.) I love encouraging others to go further, no matter what.

Mary wants everything her way, and will play with your head until she gets what it is she's after. She may say a lie and in her mind it's the truth (deep right.) She was married to her youngest child's father, which involved abuse, on a physical and mental level (as-well-as having family issues growing up) for 25 years. In the beginning of the relationship, I told her to leave her past relationship drama in the past, don't bring it into our new relationship, as-well-as me. She agreed with me and did the opposite. When we would get into an argument she would often say "been there done that." Or she would compare certain things I do to her exes, yep! If she would do something to someone, and the person would confront her on what she done, she would "flip it" and make it seem like that person did it first that's why she's doing it, and tell the individual it was all their fault . . . and it wasn't. I'm really, not trying to bash her (just telling it like it is), but she's art work.

Now, about this time two years had gone by, I was on to her games and still learning, and she didn't like it, not one bit, because I was throwing it back at her. I picked up on her patterns and the way her thoughts were at this time in our relationship.

We still enjoyed going out and being together, which was dying slowly, but our sex was still in full swing which was the glue to keeping us together, otherwise we would have parted the first year.

She hated when I told her, her games didn't work on me as much anymore. After the second year I stayed in the relationship to try and let her know who the man was, regardless of her ability to confuse people, and I mean a lot of people (and that was because she was confused in her own mind.)

We talked about growing in the beginning of the relationship, and what we need to do to get there.

One day after we had sex (earlier in the relationship) I suggested that we write down all the things in the relationship that we dislike about each other and all of the things we like. Because I really wanted to get this relationship off to a good start. So if we would go far (at the time not knowing what kind of person she was) we would make a good pitch at it, because we would have a blue print of where we need to correct our behavior, and it was on paper. Both of our good points out weighted the bad.

Now all we had to do was work diligently on each of our bad points, which is some of the things I already mentioned about myself. But in the beginning she didn't try at all (I felt.) She wanted me to do all the changing while she stayed the same. NOPE!

Years later (after we abandoned the blue print, un-knowingly) she would tell me that my shit stunk and that

I should change (which I am always willing to do for the sake of progress, in anything), but she wasn't looking in the mirror as I suggested, otherwise I would have seen change in the area of disturbance, that I pointed out to her.

If there is something about me that I need to deal with, I always look in the mirror and talk to that other side of me (mentally.) Look myself in the eyes to deal with the reality of the situation. And then go tackle whatever it is that's eating me away or holding me back.

She's not much on dealing with what's real, but I'm a realist and I'm gonna tell it to a person the way it is, whether they like it or not, that includes myself, that's the purpose of talking to myself in the mirror, or brainstorming my faults and weaknesses. It don't matter as-long-as I deal with what's real and what's not, again for the sake of progress.

So I used to tell her thing she didn't want to hear, or what other people close to her didn't want to say to her, because they know she wouldn't accept the reality of it, which may cause other problems they didn't want to deal with, so they left her in her own world.

I would say to her, "this is not your world BooBoo" she hated that. I didn't care; I was throwing reality at her, which she couldn't deal with. I wanted to help her with her issues so we could go far, as I did with my kids mother while we were in the beginning stages of that relationship.

Back to Mary. In time I began to know her even more and began to tell her what was and wasn't happening.

She wasn't feeling that. If we would get into a petty dispute talking on the cell, I would do what she would do to me, and that's hang up in her face and later let her know how it felt to have that done to you.

So she would come out with, "I don't want to be with you anymore," but still call me. Little did she know I was planning to leave her, but on my own terms, as I said in the beginning, I knew we weren't going to last.

Most of this was about my pride, and observing and learning so I would know how to deal with future game players such as her. I wasn't worried about wasting time in my life, I wanted the experience, and she was a big challenge. Women and marriage will be there, getting married for a man is no problem.

I was in my late forties, but according to other people I looked pretty good, and most, most, of all, I felt magnificent, so I didn't sweat time.

Mary was slowly beginning to humble up. She was getting older, and it began to show. She also was into one man at a time; she wasn't into multiple men, which also contributed to her humbleness. As-well-as my "persistent, uncooperative, stubbornness," by not allowing her to do what she wanted . . . when she wanted. But with the head games she's capable of, anything was possible with her.

If she got angry and upset, nasty, nasty things would come from her mouth that would really hurt someone, but she cared not, she had to express the anger she had, and if anyone got in her way she would subject them to a verbal onslaught. She needed control, to cover for her internal insecurities.

She was no longer allowed to stay at my home, because she would go through my things to get information on me, so when she got angry at me, she could tell me she had certain private information about me she could use against me like: My social security number. She also checked out what was on my pay stub, and did all this when I would leave to work.

Not once did I ever think about doing anything like that to her, even when I slept over her house, I just didn't think in that manner.

She was an extremely insecure person and would not own up to it.

Well going on the fourth year . . . that's what I said, four years of dealing with her psychological head games. I was free from any and every negative thing she came up with in order to make me feel confused.

I would tell her, her games are dead, so why continue to try. But she would, with no results to her liking.

When I wouldn't comply with her game she would get angrier and cuss me at times. At this time in our off and on relationship, I began to get nicer and kinder to her. She was no longer allowed to spend my money and save hers. I would pay for almost everything, because I felt sorry for her, she would always say that she had no money because she wasn't working.

That line stopped working about the second year, I would tell her to get a job and you would have money, and we would have a stronger relationship. She waited for other incomes from other sources to help with her bills and her life style of dressing.

At this time . . . everything became half; she would call me cheap-o. I told her, well I'm just going to be cheap because you're going to reach in your pocket and pay with me, unless I decide to pay for you.

In time she began to see nothing was working for her, and started to humble up even more, but at this time I was planning to move on without her in my life.

She needs help and wasn't about to go for it. I was beginning to turn the tide and get up in her head. Now she was slowly talking to me like she was beginning to wear out.

When I would say something that was against what she had in mind, it was now, "Okay baby" or she would say, "but why daddy", or just suck her teeth if she was in disagreement. No back talk or phone being hung up any more. It was a change, not a drastic change, but change, I'll take it.

Our relationship was still dominated by crazy good sex. We weren't seeing each other often anymore (I dictated that.) I would tell her to "do her," when she would run that I'm going out with my friend crap (She wanted me to assume it was a guy.) She didn't like me playing her game as she did, and began telling me even more, she wanted out of the relationship, because I was playing her game as-well-as she.

She said I was the best lover she ever had, and knew it would be hard to replace me in that sense.

I was willing to be just friends to her. Our communication was shrinking fast, and we were ready to go our separate ways. I felt free from her nuttiness, and was able to sleep at night, no matter what she texted or said on my cell about me, which was difficult for me to endure before. She loved me a lot, but had a strange way of showing it. She'd tell me she was going to leave me, and still, e-mail or text me, with her games.

Now, once I'm able to sleep at night and not be trippin over a woman, I can move on, and that's just what I did. I prayed (and pray) for her and wished good things for her, she would cuss me and wish the worse for me and people close to me because she wasn't getting her way.

I felt at peace and was ready for my next relationship when it came along, no rush.

I will not allow psychological head games towards me. Our relationship won't work, and I had a lot of them, it's just that Mary was the ultimate challenge. But I pray never to go through that again with a woman; it will be over in no time.

I've dealt with many women in my life who have had mental problems (I can see them a mile away, even past the phony smile), and don't want to face it, some may die without getting the help they need because they don't want people getting up in their heads and reading them; they will be forever unhappy, until they wise up.

God bless them all (people who are like that), and I really mean that. A lot of their problems come from their upbringing and lack of family love and it's also a part of their personality . . . which is another book.

Chapter 7

Handle it

One day my boss who is a Filipino asked me if I was still going with Mary (Mary would call and she would hear my conversation.) I didn't need Mary going at it with me on the phone giving those people on my job things to talk about concerning me; I was already dealing with some back stabbing people.

Dealing with the job and at times going home, then dealing with her was a lot for me, not to mention my kids and their issues. I talked to God and absorbed the bull that was transpiring around me. I did things to relax, like go dancing, or going to my room and sitting on my bed and thinking, sorting out my out of control thoughts that consumed my brain.

Good sex, then hours of sleep helps me to cope. If it is that intense of a problem, talking to someone who can give me good feedback helps. It's an ingredient of things to help me deal with stress, and depression (as I said, I don't really get depressed.)

Always remember people, Jehovah, and Jesus, are number one when dealing with the unknown, they are the best stress relievers. Saying the right things and being around the right people will also help. Dealing with my job increases my stress, if I have some at the time (most of the time I'm stress free. I may get quiet, but I'm sound on the inside.)

On the job, some of my bosses mess with me for some reason. I brought it to the attention of the director and there seemed to be amnesia or just plain old denial about everything concerning me.

Or, on certain days we have mandatory meetings and certain people would not attend, nothing is done or said. Let me or someone else they feel they can pick on go against the rules, they will be ready to pull us to the side and let us have it.

I have learned to not allow people on my job, to get the best of me. I use to hold in the injustice and allow it to build up in me until I let it out in a negative manner and be sent home or get written up.

So I changed my whole attitude towards my work environment. I take things that really don't mean anything to me with a grain of salt, **"it is what it is."** I push it to the side, in my mind, and occupy my thoughts with something more important and meaningful that needs to be attended to, this can be better said than done, you must believe and practice.

I'm searching for ways to do better in life and get out of that environment, something pertaining to kids and making a difference to others. If my boss docks me for being out of the area, and others do it, but they feel they can mess with me (dock means to take money away from you); I don't argue and run to the union to rectify the problem, I take it as a grain of salt, especially if it's my fault.

I shake my head look them in the eye (not with anger but in a relaxed manner), and give them a piece of my mind . . . "respectfully," in a calm manner, to get it off my chest, so it won't linger in my brain heavily and then turn away from them and leave.

If you are wrong, one must learn to accept their faults and not argue. Don't be wrong and strong like a lot of us do. Make sure you don't put yourself in that situation again.

When I come across situations like that or similar, I do what I think is right and keep it moving. I always replace negative thoughts with positive ones. I try to keep my mind clear of anger and frustration. Keep my heart rate and pressure down by not getting excited.

Now if you find yourself in a tough uncontrollable situation, try, try, try and relax. Breathe deep, breath relax, and try to focus on one thought at a time (I know better said than done.) Too many thoughts going through your mind confuses you and could make the heart rate speed up, your blood pressure goes up, your mind loses a grip on everything, and you may find yourself regretting your actions, some people call it "blacking out," if it gets to that level.

Think positive, and say things like . . . *I'm good.*

I will not allow this individual, or situation to get the best of me (or whatever). Listen to the person talk, absorb everything, say what you need to say and step. If there are individuals on the job you do not like, keep them at a distance.

If they are not a kind person stay away from them, especially if it's not job related (try and be respectful, and humble, that helps keep your stress down), those individuals are equal to stress.

If you want to, say good morning, to show that person and everyone else that you are the better person, (that's a big plus in God's eyes), do so and keep it moving. Taking this step makes you feel good on the inside, even if you are ignored; you did what God wanted and reached out.

DO NOT HATE!!!

Hate is like a cancer. It will slowly, slowly take its toll on you, especially if you dislike a number of people. So don't let your job environment or any place (even home) get the best of you and make you go against who you are as an individual and take you out of your character. When I come to work in the morning, and there are people I like and people I don't see eye-to-eye with. I greet all at once . . . **"Good morning everybody!!!"** I'd say.

Know yourself and what makes you angry, and learn how to calm yourself down. If you are a hot head, and get angry quickly, practice, practice, practice (again, breathing deeply can help, somewhat, but not totally.)

If you don't, your anger will get the best of you one day, and you will regret your actions. If need be, bite your pride and take anger management courses.

If someone tries to intentionally make you upset, look at them, smile, and keep moving, keep that up and in time they will feel defeated and will begin to wonder about you. Believe me if they can't rent out space in your head (make you do what they want you to do), they will begin to change their outlook towards you.

If you are constantly being harassed, tell that person (alone) that you don't appreciate what they are trying to do, and if it continues, you will go to management or whoever is in charge and report them, do it in a stern but controlling manner. Don't allow anything in this world to stress you out, because again stress leads to depression, which takes you to another level and contribute to your body breaking down.

Getting back to Mary, the more I ignored her childish mind games the more upset she became. I let her know that I'm not going to be a feather in her cap, "go play with your next man's head," I would say. I was living at my brother's house at the time. We had just moved in with him his wife and kids, some time ago.

We left my sons friend mothers home, who happens to be raising 5 foster care children, one girl and four boys my sons age, and a little older.

We had to leave there because all the kids began to get into arguments which was stressing the foster care mother out (may God bless her heart for allowing us to be there for the amount of time we were . . . . **THANK YOU!** She is a very strong woman with physical ailments, and dealt with those hard headed kids), and we agreed on a certain amount of months for us to live there anyway.

I had nowhere to go, so I began to think about going onto the shelter system "again," all the long, I thought I lost my Sec.8 because I was thrown out by the land lord, in which we went through the court system in order for me to leave.

So my son had brought up to my sister in law (bless her) that we were about to make another appearance into the system, and she allowed us to stay at her house until I was able to get on my feet, so we moved in immediately.

My brother is younger than me. He has 2 boys, about my sons' age and 2 a little older, plus a younger daughter about 4 years of age. My brother and his wife have a great relationship, I wish I could find a woman to bond with like that; she's a good woman, dedicated to her man, and family.

They've been together for over 20 years and more and I've never heard them argue, not one time, that's awesome, I like that. She works and takes care of the whole house, my brother is a good man as well, he wants no problems just to live a simple life and indulge in sports.

In time we had to leave there as well because they needed room, and we were taking that up. My eldest son lived with his mother at the time because she became sickly. And I told him he is the oldest, so it was his responsibility to stay there and care for this mother, while his brothers and I went into the system.

Chapter 8

Merry-go-round

I put whatever else I had into the storage and took what I needed into the system. Once we got to the new E.A.U. building now called *"Path"* (which was rebuilt.)

It was no longer one level (years ago it was one floor, including the lower level), but about 5 stories high. I was like wow, it was totally different. We walked up the walk way. We meaning my youngest and middle child, into the building and waited on the long line to get checked for weapons, or anything that can be used as a weapon.

Then we did intake, and from there to the elevators to the second floor for more questions and answers.

There we got lucky and found some seats (ha-ah, hey) in the crowd, and we waited for our number or name to be called, which was a boring process.

Patience is needed, otherwise you would bug out. It was mostly populated with women and children, Hispanics and blacks. Blacks tipping the scale as we always do when it comes mostly to negative things.

Sisters bitching about how slow things were, making a scene. But the D.H.S. police and security "ain't havin' it," they will arrest you if you do not cooperate. After a while my kids got hungry. I had no money at the time, but even if I did and left the building to feed them, when we came back we'd had to get searched again etc. and that was a process I didn't want to go through. I was told to go down stairs to eat, as I saw around me people with brown bags, with food in them, like: Milk, a ham and cheese sandwich, cookies, apples, just enough to hold you over.

It was not like my first time coming into the system. This food was actually better I felt.

I had to leave the second floor and go to the lower level to get the food. There was no line like before.

Now, you walk up to the guy sign your name and he gives you what you want, as-much-as you want . . .

Cool!

Once I got what I needed, I went back upstairs (before they called my name) and gave my sons their bags. In time my number was called to see the worker who was to interview me. After that I was told to wait for my number to be called to go to the next level, which was the 4th floor, the welfare floor.

Once there, I waited some more for a couple of hours, "that's right you heard me" . . . **HOURS!!**

After I was called and interviewed, I was then told to go back down to the next level, the exit level, where I got the food. Once there, we again got lucky and found three more seats in a more crowded environment.

It was over crowded because people were leaving to get placed in their 10 day shelter as well! Once in a ten day shelter you had to be eligible, in order to be placed in a tier two shelter, so you could move on and find an apartment.

The last level was crazy. My middle son Akeem and I sat and bonded (talked) while my youngest son Ahmaud played with the other shelter bound children.

After a couple of more hours of waiting my number was called and the worker at the counter gave me an address to where I was to go, which was Bedford Stuyvesant, Brooklyn, and told me I had a choice on how to get there.

I had a choice to get metro cards for me and my sons and take the train, or, take a bus that they provided. But, I had my van, and we got to our destination quickly. Before I left I asked them if it was possible for me to be placed in a shelter in Queens, which would put me in the borough my youngest son went to school.

It was said that D.H.S. will send you to a shelter where your youngest son goes to school, to make it easier on the parent and child.

They said that I must get past my 10 day assessment, investigation, and then I can make that type of request, for him to go to a school in a certain area of my desire.

Well, we left Path and went about our business to the Brooklyn shelter. Once we got there we went through another intake, which took about 20 minutes. After that they gave me the key to my apartment, which was a two bed room, kitchen, and living room that was huge. They gave me sheets for the beds, and we went right to sleep about 12:00 am.

The next day we had to visit the social workers office to give them more information about us. Once that was done, I when to buy food for my boys and went back to my storage space in Queens to get pillows and other needed things.

This particular shelter I lived didn't even look like a shelter on the outside at all. It looked like a regular apartment building, compared to the past shelters I lived.

I wasn't interested in any woman (I was dealing with Shell at the time and that's it.)

Unlike my last visit to the shelter, I was single and up in everything. Now my mindset is not on those things, it was on getting in the shelter and getting out . . . **STRICTLY**! A couple of women who were there began to come on to me. One on my floor had three kids and said she would come by to visit me and hang out . . . hang out, ha-ha, yeah right! There was nothing they could do to suck me in, I handled the temptation well, and didn't allow things to get to me. I was a stepper all the way; I wasn't interested in getting to know no one. I'd come in late and leave early (as steppers do), like about 5:00 am. I'd get dressed then wake up the boys, they'd get dressed and we hopped in my van and head straight to the Jackie Robinson parkway to get to Queens, or take the J train to the last stop, which were about 17 stops. I dropped my sons off at their needed destinations, and jet to my job. I wanted my baby to stay in Queens, without going to school in Brooklyn. He knew everyone in the school he was presently in, and the teachers worked with him well.

If he would go to a new school, it would throw him off in class for one, plus, he had to get accustomed to being in a new environment, around new kids. I didn't want him in nothing new; it would offset his flow and bring down his grades I worked so hard to get up.

After I dropped my baby off, I would park my car somewhere near the subway to make things easy for me, as-far-as me not paying to get on the bus, to get to the subway. Coming back was only a couple of blocks to walk.

Once I got off from work, I would pick my baby son up at the park, and go take care of whatever business I needed to with him with me.

I met my second oldest son at the library so he could study on days he didn't have football practice, or, I'd give him some space and let him hang with his friends. We'd make plans for us to meet wherever, or he would (at times) come back to the shelter in Brooklyn by train, and I'd meet him there. He was older so he was flexible.

I am a hard dad, especially when it comes to school. I believe black people aren't hard enough on our kids. This is one of the reasons why a large portion of our kids are not graduating from high school the way they are supposed to and going to college. High School is the beginning of the steppin' stone to success. Now, once we got back to the shelter which was usually about 9 or 10 o'clock, we'd then eat and get ready for the next day. Remember it's the beginning of the school year so there wasn't as much homework being given, but it would be done if any was.

I teach my boys independence so they won't have to depend on no one but themselves.

In the shelter I now reside, they had monthly meetings about what is going on in there and gave my sons school supplies.

You can't come in when you wanted because they had a curfew which was at 10:00 pm. If you are late, you can still come in, it's just that you get written up and a warming letter is slipped under your apartment door.

If you stayed out for that night, you must be back within 48 hours from the time you left, or you would get logged out and Path (who runs everything) will take your apartment away from you.

Now one must go back to Path in the Bronx and start the whole process of intake again into the system.

So after living in the shelter for about two weeks, I was found ineligible to-get-to the next level (tier two.) When

I first came into the system in 1999, I was eligible on the first shot.

When I received the bad news from management at the shelter, I got my boys that evening and we went back down to Path to start all over again. I'm thinking "damn" here we go again, like a *"Merry-go-round."* I was thinking I hope I don't wind up being like the homeless people there who are taking a ride through the system, and not getting settled in order to get housing. But before I met up with my hearts (Boys), I went upstairs to my apartment and gathered everything, not knowing I would not be leaving all together. I was really upset but kept my cool, and not take it out on the staff, or my sons.

I had plastic garbage bags and begun to clean out the apartment. I took all the things that were in my room, which were clothes on the bed, my TV, and all the stuff in the kitchen which was a lot of frozen food, then went into my son's room and cleaned up in there as well.

Then, finally, the living room, where I had the most things accumulated. I took all the bags and drug them towards the door, to be ready to leave, "quickly," so when I come back to move, things will be ready. Then when I finally meet up with my boys, I don't want them to go through all that packing crap, and drain their will power I'm trying to build up (look that phrase up people, **"Will Power"** you will learn a lot, that can make a difference in your life.)

When we got to Path, I wanted to know why I was rejected, and they said they had problems with information pertaining to where I was in the last two years.

Investigators want to know where we were in that time period. So, I was told that they had problems with one of the addresses I gave, and that was the lady I stayed with for about 6 months.

I was pissed off about that because I went to her house and told her that the investigators would be coming by the house to talk to her about me living there for some time. Now I'm here because of whatever reason and didn't want to jump to conclusions until I talked with her first.

My son Akeem had her cell number, I asked him to give me the number so I could ask her what happened with her talking to the investigator, but I could not get through, as I tried patiently.

Sometimes the foster mother's cell is turned off. That's what I learned while living there.

So when we got there, it seemed like it got more crowded, with more families, which made us stay there for more hours this time around. It was harder to find seats, my sons were as upset as I was, but I encouraged them to endure and stay positive, and believe tomorrow is another day. I was trying to teach them, how to deal with issues in life without exploding, and or going over the edge. I was feeling bad that my boys had to go through all of this; it made me feel less than a good dad.

I'd tell them to believe in their father, because that was my primary function and focus, to get my sons an apartment. I told them to try and be patient throughout our entire shelter visit. I try to instill the belief in God and a positive outlook on life. In this instance, I try to teach them how to cope with different issues being thrown their way, due to uncontrollable circumstances that may arise. I was told all my things back at the Brooklyn shelter will be kept there until, or, if I come back. I thought that they would be placing us in a different shelter this go round. I was being positive and wishing I would be placed in Queens this time, closer to my son Ahmaud's School.

Then I was called by the staff at Path, to be placed again, while in the basement level (the last step before being placed into a 10 day assessment shelter.) They sent me back to the shelter I just left, I was so disappointed.

I just knew I was gone from that shelter, but that wasn't the case. They changed the process around since I was there last, in 1999.

Years ago they would have placed you in another shelter. I heard other people there being replaced as well; Path sent them back to the same shelter. Some women didn't want to go back to their last shelter and broke down and cried.

Yes, I was disappointed, but I kept moving forward knowing that everything would be ok in due time. I had endured disappointment throughout my entrance into the system, but had to hang in there for the sake of my sons (back in 2000 and now.)You're dealing with a lot of depressed, stressed, unhappy individuals and their negativity can rub off on you . . . oh yeah, it can.

Their nasty looks alone can affect you, if you allow it. So you as an individual who has goals in life (I'm talking in general now) and are a happy go lucky person, must stay positive and stay away from the miserable people and crowd that can suck you in. This is advice I'm giving my readers, not just in the shelter, but something that should be applied in other sectors of life, as well.

I talked to God often, and got sleep, which helps a down spirit and over worked body. I too took my own advice and took life a day at a time, and went with the wind, and tried not to fight it.

Circumstances against you while you fight life can burn you out, depending on how long you go against it, with your tolerance level and energy you put forth.

So we endured the pain of returning and dealing with the shelter rules.

I had to see a case worker once a week to discuss a plan for me and the boys to leave, which was what I was already doing to get out. The social worker said it didn't take much planning for me, because I had a job, and a strong desire to leave, unlike a lot of other people in the system who would like to make the system their home (Leaches.)

We also sat and filled out a computer questionnaire about my status pertaining to the system . . . again!

Hey, like I said, you have to go with the wind. All kinds of things began to happen unexpectedly during that time for me and my boys. For instance: My car decided it was going to act up now, when I needed it most. It decided to cut off on me early in the morning while I was taking my son to school. It stalled on us. Water was leaking from the bottom. So I decided we get out and walk a quarter of a mile, until we found a golf course (me and my baby son.) We then found containers, filled them up with water and proceeded back to the car. When I got back, the police were there with a tow truck, taking my van somewhere in Brooklyn, crap! Now I needed money to get my van out. I borrowed a couple of hundreds from my brother. I had to pay for the tow and each day it was on the lot, which was 35 dollars . . . daily. I got it out the next day.

When I got to work I was deeply upset but tried not to show it, I get quite when something is on my mind, and still had the ability to smile. I had to in spite of what was going on in my life, I try to stay positive.

At the time I was having big problems with my lady (Shell), she was angry at me, allowing her imagination get the best of her. She's so insecure she thought I was messing around with women in the shelter, and I kept telling her I'm a dedicated man.

So her thinking the way she did was on my mind, because I wanted her to be at ease, plus other things that needed attention in life on a minor scale that affected me (which I won't get into.)
I was a mental mess.
But I had God!

I stayed focused and didn't allow anyone on the job to get me upset, because I was deep in thought, the way my life had been at the time. I hung in there and stayed humble and committed to getting my life straight, regardless of the issues poppin' up.

Also within the shelter, I had to deal with the education lady I had to go see pertaining to my sons, what schools they were in and whether or not my baby would get bussed to Queens, as I was told.

She wanted the schools number, as-well-as the school needing to know where the kids were living at the time. I had to see her every week so she could give me and the kid's metro cards.

She would give it to me not knowing I was driving (somewhat) at the time . . . hey, I still took it, it would come in handy in the future. But in order for me to get another one, I must use the one she gave me first. She would put her name on the back, so I wouldn't switch cards.

When you leave your apartment, management is allowed to come there while you're not home, to inspect and check the condition of your apartment. If your apartment is undesirable, you have failed inspection and must get it to satisfactory.

I failed for the first time of me ever being in the system (as I said before I had a lot of things in the living room, all over the place.) Oh yeah, if you have any problems with where you live, like the area you live, or the shelter itself. You have to take that up with the management of the shelter you are living in, and ask them for a transfer. They will contact an organization called "Hero," and Hero will decide if you can get a transfer, or not. However, Path basically makes all the other decisions pertaining to you, not the shelter you are living in. As time progressed, I came to management and put in a request for a weekend pass. You get that if you abide by all the rules, a chance to leave the facilities on Friday into Sunday night, but you must return by 10:00 pm.

As time passed, my social worker (two weeks passed since I was found ineligible the first time) said to me that Path found me ineligible to stay there again, for the same reason, a problem with that foster care mother. So I called my son Akeem and instructed him to meet me at Path again. I was so upset and disappointed; I had to really focus on what I needed to do first, because I had so many things rushing through my mind at the time that needed to be addressed while at the shelter . . . I had to ask them for a seat to relax myself before I made my next move.

I needed to gather my thoughts.

That moment was really intense.

So, I went and picked up my baby son Ahmaud and we got on the train and met Akeem at Path again (I'm still upset.) I sat in McDonald's with them and asked them if they wanted to continue to go through this merry go round crap. They weren't with it, in spite of how quick I told them our stay in the system would be. I didn't want to continue to do this running around with them, so, I sat and thought . . . and thought . . . and thought.

My boys really didn't want to go live with their mother.

They didn't want to be in the Bronx where she lived for one . . . two, she runs her mouth and never stops and they are accustomed to living with their daddy most of all (I'm fair.) I finally told them I had nowhere else to take them, I must call their mother and see if they can stay with her, until I got us an apartment, and in a six month time period, that I did.

Chapter 9

Adjust

I gave my boys to their mother and had to move in at the time with Mary . . . ***MAN! I know, I know people, be easy on me, please!***

I had a family van, and would drive her and pick her up from where ever she liked while there, because that's me, I love to pamper my lady.

I bought food, gave money, anything to do my part (that's what a man is supposed to do, care for his woman, his family and if necessary his community.)

We went washing. I was trying to make it work still, being that I was staying at her mother's house with her. We'd have laughing moments often.

I'd get up go to work, get off, and go do my thing to get an apartment. I would call her to let her know where I was and what was up (remember I live with her, so I must play by her rules or . . . .)

I'm with letting my lady know where I am anyway; and she did the same with me.

She calls most of the time, until she flips. So it went both ways.

We didn't have money so we couldn't do much, but watch movies. I wanted us to spend time playing X-Box, but she gets upset when things don't go her way, and my X-Box would have been sitting in the street.

She's a good person as well, when she's not under any pressure . . . let me get that straight.

Now when I would have problems with my kid's mother, she would get upset with me and tell me go to her, she didn't want any baby mama drama, which is understandable. But she'd sit and release all the issues she had penned up in her about both of her kids' fathers, yep, she's unreal.

Yes I had problems with my kid's mother as well. I gave her my boys for a couple of months. Because I moved from my brother's house into my woman's home in the basement, until I found an apartment. They couldn't come, so I had to convince their mother to take her kids for a couple of months, until I got on my feet. Yeah, you heard, "CONVINCE." For the whole 16 years plus I had the children, my kid's mother never gave me a dime, from the time I got them from her, back in early 1998 . . . not a dime *"ya hurd!"* She was demanding that I give her $300 every two weeks in order for her to take her kids (I know, I know Mr. Parks where in the hell do you find your women, you ask?)

I agreed to it, and it was written down on a piece of paper. Because if I didn't, she may not have taken them and that would have put me in a real bind. In reality, in the back of my mind I was thinking yeah right you think you gonna get that amount from me, you are truly buggin.

She too is a good person (when she's not stressed), she loves to cook, she respects the crap out of her parents, but she has a drinking issue that hurts her as a person. It's all about money for her, even when it comes to her kids, she's not working, and depends on men, and, the government to care of her.

She wanted to take the boys for three months, but when she found out that she can get SSI from the government for my baby son, she decided that she wanted to now keep them (especially him) a little longer, which never happened.

When I had the boys she wasn't thinking, I have kids let me work at least part time and help their father out with them to make life easier. I took her to court for some money but she wasn't working and they didn't put pressure on her to do so (Double standard when it comes to women, which needs to change.)

My kid's mother doesn't think like that, she's like Mary and wants a free ride. When you attract a certain type of individual, it's hard to change the pattern, help is needed for me. Like certain people attract, or are attract ed to people who are abusive, or, people who cheat. My kid's mother has physical ailments, it wasn't as bad years ago, but because she has not taken care of herself and getting older, she is getting worse. She is sicker than she was five years ago and was working then.

I'm not angry as I was years ago, I learned to let it go and do for the boys on my own, as-long-as my father above sees the love to drive them in the right direction, that's all that matters to me, as of now. My mother told me to do the same thing years ago, and I listened, but with me struggling with babies was hard to do and still is.

However, with maturity, I've learned to not cry over spilled milk and keep moving, until I do and get where I want to be in life, it's the past! Just keep your head up and gradually take steps toward the future you seek, understand people.

Back to main topic.
So one day I left work and stopped by the real estate office to see if they had anything for me. After that I stopped by the store to pick up some juice for her boys because they go through juice like it's nothing. I had already called her up and let her know that I was going to do these things. Once I got to the house and came down the stairs she was there cleaning, giving me the stare down, as she begun to accuse me of things I had no idea what she was talking about *(readers let me straighten something out . . . NOW, I deal with one woman at a time; I have never, ever, given her any reason to think that I was unfaithful or anything like* that, she's full of insecurities . . . . PERIOD!)

At this time I became sick of her insecurities and gave her my don't mess with me look. One thing led to another and she told me I could get all my stuff and leave. It was

November 14, 2012, and very cold outside, however, I didn't care. I had to let her know that she wasn't going to think she could do as she pleased with me because I was living temporarily under her roof (sometimes in life people you have to sacrifice in order to make a point, or get to another level, fact.)

I told her to get all my stuff, I was cool and calm, I'd been through this with her before. Once I got my stuff, even food in the freezer and refrigerator, I walked out the door. I had a ring on my finger she bought, so she can feel like she's married. I left that on the top step as I was leaving; she called it an engagement ring, I call it a commitment ring, she didn't like that, but as I said, she's not running this relationship, period it's not happening.

Chapter 10

Homeless

Now, I was homeless, seriously homeless, but I would not go back, as-cold-as it was, I would have to man up and deal. I would try to live and survive out of my van for a while. I have clothing in the back seat, food in the miniature cabinets. Things I needed to get me by for the time being, until I found me an apartment.

I slept in my van for that night but the cold was unbearable, I got no sleep at all. The next day I called my grandmother and asked her if I could stay there until I found an apartment. And of course grandparents are always there for you. My grandmother, *hahahahah*, I wouldn't switch her for no one in the world, lord as my witness, I love her so much.

Now let me tell you people about this great woman . . . . she is 87 years of age. Born in Saint Louis, she basically raised 12 children by herself. I say basical ly because, my grandfather who I talked about in my last book **"SHELTERED"** was a great man (who is a part of our American history, that's what I mean when I say great) but a play boy, who was there but wasn't. Three days he was home and five he wasn't, hypothetically speaking. So my beautiful grandmother did most of the work. My grandfather gave money bought food, cleaned around the house, yes he did, help discipline us all, with a positive impact. My grandmother, however, did most of the upbringing that trumped my grandfather, because of the lack of time he was home. They had 5 boys and 6 girls, and she raised a granddaughter from an aunt who passed away.

She's truly an amazing person!

Love for all her blood . . . no favoritism for none, everyone gets the same treatment. She went to college and finished in her late 50s, graduated and went on to teach and also worked with children at Martin de Porres. She, my mother and grandfather influenced me to be the best I can be (wait as I dry the tears from my eyes, "sniff, sniff" this is so emotional for me) and to reach for your goal no matter what age you are, as-long-as you're healthy, you can achieve what you believe, if you have the ambition and drive. I love and thank them for instilling that in my mind, body and soul.

My grandmother lives with my mother and sister in the same house but different apartments in Brooklyn. My mother who is a wonderful person who also worked while raising three kids in her late thirties finished college. She now works daily, travels often, and is not home much. So I began to stay with my grandmother who lived in the basement (See her picture in last pages of this story.)

She is sickly and needs nursing. So while I was there I did what she would allow me to do for her, for she is very independent. I would stay with her on a daily basis for some time while taking care of my responsibilities . . . until. She had to take time off and go to Maryland to see my other side of the family, and a doctor, pertaining to her health.

I was again faced with the dilemma of getting a roof over my head. I would stay with the woman whom I had a shady relationship with, but that wasn't concrete.

I could also go to my brother's house, which was big and roomy.

There were times, for some reason, I got to the house late (about 11, everyone goes to bed early) and my brother would have worked over night at his job. I was forced to sleep in my van, in the cold, nice right.

I slept in my cold van quite a few times while being homeless with nowhere to go. Being homeless effects how you begin to look at yourself. If people don't want you around because you're jobless and homeless you begin to look inward and question yourself.

I had family turn me down, just because I was homeless. I didn't steal and had a good relationship with them . . . Family Ha-Ha!

Because of my situation, they turned me away for that night. I dressed well, with clean clothing, my mind has all its marbles (at least I, I, I think), I had a job, I drove. I was able to feed myself without asking for food. I was good as-far-as those things were concerned. I got up early to go to work and took care of anything that was needed, so I wasn't lying around the house or being lazy.

However, people are funny, certain family members as well. Let me give you an example:

I have this family member whom I love deeply and had a good relationship with turn me down from staying at his house for one night. He was a pioneer of Hip Hop, a somewhat big name in the industry.

When I was in my teens he would bring me to his shows back in the early eighties. We would be all over New York, he was down with the Disco Twins, who were well known back then and even now, although they never got over that hump and became known throughout America.

I would meet all the big named rappers and deejays, such as Dee Jay Hollywood, Deejay Starsky, Deejay Smalls, Deejay Eddie Chebba, all big named people who didn't get to the level as Run-DMC, and LL Cool J. I mean these guys would rock the house. If you had a soul, then you would be moving your hips, they were that nice. I had influence all around me to be a big time rapper, as Whitney Houston had big time singers all around her to inspire her to be a soul singer from her mother and aunt, when she was a little girl (however that wasn't my future which is another story.)

So, I had a good relationship with my this family member, he was like my big brother. He was about three years older than me. When my mother brought me to see my grandma he was the one I looked forward to seeing, as a youngster. When there was a blizzard outside he would ask me to go out with him and shovel people's cars and drive ways, make walkways in front of their stores or houses. So, you have an idea of how much he impacted my life as-well-as my elders (parents), he was a go getter, a shaker.

So one day it was cold outside and I had nowhere else to go. So, I called my favorite uncle to see if I could stay over his house for that night, only. I'd been to his house one time prior to asking him that day, and that was about three to four years ago. He said to me that I never called to ask to come over before, or even speak to him (Which was true), the answer was . . . NO!!

I was somewhat surprised even though he's a grouchy person, and very cheap. But I was thinking [we have love for each other], it's cold outside, and I have nowhere else to go for the night, but to sleep in my van. He turned me down "cruelly" with no remorse, yep!

He said this is the only time you call me just to stay at my house (we do/did see each other at family events throughout the years), and he made up an excuse and said his son was at his house that night (who's only about 12 years old and has his own room.) I told him so what, I have covers and things I need, I just needed a warm place to sleep just for the night. I will sleep on the floor anywhere; and will be up to go to work in the morning. He still turned me down and check this out folks . . . he hung the phone up on my face, **POW!** AHA!

I was like WOW! I couldn't believe it. Now I do understand that I called just to stay there for that night only, and I should have come to see him in the past, yes, yes, yes he's right. However people, I'm family in need, striving in life, not waiting for things to come to me, working to get it, to be the best I can be, he's aware of this.

He could have said, I'm not happy with you calling just to stay at my house for the night "DOG," however, I will let you stay here on the floor (or wherever), just for this night; find somewhere else to stay in the future.

Remember people we have a good relationship, and most of all, it was cold outside, you could see your breath, chilly cold. I had to sleep in the cold that night, again with very little sleep. He let me down, big time. I could have gotten sick with a cold, or even pneumonia and die. I was angry at him as I thought on it. He was right; I should have visited him more in the past. I still think he could have allowed me to stay for that night; I talked to God and made mental efforts to forgive him, and I do, although I will never see him the same.

I know who I am and what I'm all about . . . my goals in life and direction, and my family members are aware of this as well. However, when you have family (outside of others) reject you, coupled with the fact that you have the same clothing on for days (not me, other homeless people), and not put water on your body for a while. Begging like you never have before, in order to survive, sets your mindset back, and makes you ashamed, which begins to reset your thinking patterns, rewires your mind, as you slowly lose confidence in yourself, and who you are . . . somewhat quickly! Now, your self esteem takes a turn for the worst each day you live in this manner, until you begin to lose more confidence in yourself (if you are not strong), especially, if you have no goals, as you begin to listen to the negativity other people have to say. I found myself tasting this state of mind, although I knew me and know I have goals in mind, and that this way of life was a test for me, nothing more. God puts us through many tests in life, to see and make us stronger.

This negative mind set could not go far with me, although others who are in this situation with nothing (no assets lack of human communication) can quickly fall victim to its gripping effects. As time when on I continued to visit other family members in New York, killing time, as homeless people do, and staying warm, until I found me a place to live, which in due time I knew I would.

Again I believe God was testing me, knowing what I am aiming at in life, so I would get a taste and understand life on the streets being homeless. I now understand how it feels by not sleeping in a warm bed at night, and not get a warm meal to help you sleep. If I didn't find a place to get quality sleep for that night, where ever I was, I'd start my van up, and drive to a parking spot near the subway station, try to sleep (I only drive to work on weekends), so in the early morning I could walk to the subway station and make it easy for me, financially. Sometimes I would have work clothing already at the job. Endure some of the daily phoniness at work, block it out and stay to myself, "somewhat." At times I had no place to go, so I would stay longer after work, or go to the job library and type this book in my spare time, taking advantage of the extra time.

Some days after I left the hospital, I did two things, I would go to the real-estate so they could help me find an apartment, staying positive knowing something would come as-soon-as Jesus was ready to provide me. Or, I would go to the gym to keep myself healthy (which was on the job as well) so I could live out my dreams and help other needy individuals.

I would be in the library at different times, depending on what I had to do. While there I would read, write, type, and print out important papers for me to go over, whatever it was. As said, after the library I would hit the gym. After that I would go to the lounge area and eat my hospital food I got from my department or food I bought from the store. Look at the sports channel, maybe a movie, and get a little shut eye for a while. Many times not knowing where I would be sleeping once I left the job.

Not a nice situation to be in people!

I would try not to run out my welcome by having who ever see my face unnecessarily daily looking for shelter, I try to avoid it. I never slept in the hospital overnight; I would leave the hospital around 10:00 or 11:00pm. There were many times I would go to the public library and stay there until closing (9:00pm), then go to Burger King, eat, and write some more (again, killing time) and then go to my destination for that night where ever that may be (most likely my brothers) I hated my situation, but . . .
I was grateful it wasn't worse.
I was grateful to have a job.
I was grateful to be able to eat, and to wash.

Thank you Jesus!

It was cold out, and I had it better that most homeless people on the streets. I was still blessed! And still thinking on a high level of advancement and I wasn't going to allow nothing or no body to interfere with that frame of mind, to hell with "MISERY LOVES COMPANY", misery wasn't getting no part of me, ha-ha.

If you're in a situation where you have no place to go, talk to God and take it a day at a time, do what you need to do in order to get yourself out of that situation, so you won't deteriorate, mentally, physically and spiritually by not being in sync with the rotating earth and heavenly bodies around you. And not feel and love yourself, by allowing people who "God said" not to trust dictate your thinking, and have you believe that you are something, or someone, that you're not. Again, you must know who you are and not allow anyone to disturb that type of way you are wired.

If you are homeless with no hope, think about the time when you were a child, or teenager, and remember the things you wanted. Well you can still shoot for your dreams and goals, by keeping your eyes on the prize. Convince yourself that in order for me to get what I want, I must first have a job (even if it's a McDonald's job.) Hey, you have to start from somewhere.

Getting a job is paramount, because that is the foundation to build.

Now, you can get a roof over your head, and a room if need be. At this point, you can begin to plan your next step towards whatever it is you want, but there must be effort, not just talking to God and things appear, like many of us do. You must work with him in order to accelerate the process . . . make sense?

Now, with a roof over your head, you can buy clothing, make yourself look presentable and have some kind of money in your pocket. Now your esteem begins to blossom. You now have the confidence to move further towards your goal (whatever it may be.) If you can move up in position, even to supervisor in McDonald's or where ever you are working, and try to feel a little better about yourself, that would be a plus before you leave that job and go after your ultimate goal.

Remember that everything is gradual, "step-by-step," just like a baby learning to crawl, then walk, then trot, and before you know it, he's running to catch the house cat (which will happen in time because that's what he wants to accomplish.) It will take time, but you must want to shoot for what you desire, and be patient, knowing that you will get there. Remember our most powerful father didn't build earth in one day, it was a process . . . hello! Whatever you believe you can achieve, starting at the point where you are. You are never too old to start, remember my grandmother started college in her mid fifties, and completed four years, why because she was determined to turn her life around and make a difference to others.

No matter how small or silly others, or, you may think it is, go for it. You must want to achieve so much that its burns like a forest fire within you. It should be something you wake up thinking about, and think about most of the day. Like a new job, or a new boyfriend or girlfriend, that's how much you should want to grow.

Anyway, I would talk to God as-much-as I could, and ask him to give me the strength to go out and make things happen.

As for the people who are miserable and want you to feel like them, or, who say you can't do this or do that. Use that negative energy they give off to fuel your non existent, or minor desires to shut them up. To prove them wrong. Do what they said you can't do.

The only difference I had over paupers who slept in the streets was the fact that, I was protected from instant physical harm. By me living in my van, I was protected (to a degree) from someone putting their hands on me. From the rain, the snow, the elements. When I would leave my job, I had to think about where I was going to rest my head that evening, where would I iron my clothing and shower. Even though most on the list aren't much of a worry, the fact that I had to think about it was disturbing to me, because I never had to think on that level before. Now imagine what the people on the streets have to go through. These people needed help, and when a person needs help in bolstering their esteem, especially a family member, you should have a humane response to care.

Anyway, I'm fortunate to have a large family and for someone to be there for me. I will have my boys back into my life as-soon-as I find a place. I started the job, and even if I didn't want to, I will finish it. I wasn't going to give them to their mother and jet for good. They wouldn't be the same kids as opposed to the way I begun to raise them.

Their mother is more into her men than she is her children. When I call them, they tell me that they are having problems with their mother (because of the drinking at times) or her boyfriend. They could not stay there; they would find themselves in the street just to get away from their mother and her nonsense.

Well in time Mary allowed me back into her house, Ha-Ha, I knew it would be a matter of time before that happened. Remember that, when you're homeless people, you take what you can get. Time went on and by the time I knew it, she threw my ass out again (for petty reasons I won't get into.) I'm praying and hopping that the sooner I find an apartment the sooner I will dispel of this gypsy type of life style I'm living. For the time being I needed every warm shelter I can have, so I can be comfortable and rest, to prevent me from going to my last resort . . . **"Sleeping in my van."**

I will continue to do the same routine daily, until life begins to bounce my way.

That means, going to the gym in order to stay healthy, so when things do go my way and my objective are in sight, I will be in good shape and able to handle it.

And going to the library to-continue-to pursue my purpose, which is another.

Yo, Yo, check this out. Remember I told you guys how I lost my Sec.8 Well allow me to tell you about the lord and how he can and will answer ones prayers, in time. I prayed to God that things would get better for me and my boys, and I hurry up and get an apartment, wishing that I still had my Section 8.

Well one day I went to my eldest uncle's house (not the one who screwed me over) where my mail was being received, who I have not been visiting to for a while. I began going through all my mail when all of a sudden I came across an envelope from Section 8 housing. I instantly opened it, like a kid opening his present on X-Mas. They were telling me the things I needed to bring to them in order to maintain their services. I'm thinking, "Oh crap, I'm still on" I wrote them off months ago, I thought they terminated me for good, because I couldn't prove that I paid the landlord her money from the rent paying apartment I last resided with my boys.

So, the next day I took the letter down to the office to see what the H.E.L.L. they were writing about.

The worker told me that they sent me a letter stating that I had a briefing (that's when they talk to you about what's needed in order to get and move into your apartment.) I was like "what the," I wasted no time in filling out the necessary papers, handed them in and waited for the results, as I crossed my fingers. It was weeks since I was supposed to-go-to my briefing . . . according to my letter. At this time I could be terminated.

I left it to God and went back to my homeless life. Things were looking up for me, because around that time I found an apartment (not through city.) I had "just" gone down to welfare to get what they call a one shot deal a couple of days ago. That's when welfare lends you money to get you into the apartment of your choice; you must pay them back, of course.

They provide you with whatever amount you need. Once that deal went through I was basically in. But now that I have my Sec. 8 back into my life, all that is a void. In three days the Sec. 8 lady called me and said that I was approved. Now I can begin to look for a Sec.8 apartment, "immediately." I must come back to the briefing they had scheduled for me in two weeks, which was due to talking to the man upstairs.

PRAYER HELPS!

Hopefully I will pay less money for rent, which will allow me to do certain things I need to do with the extra money, let's hope!

I can also take my Sec.8 to another state, as-well-as get me a house. If I was living in the projects, I could not get a house, and could not move to another state. Having Sec. 8 can help me with a brighter future and help me with my goals.

However, let's not jump the gun, I'm still homeless. How am I going to take it people? That's it, one day at a time. I still have a while to go, and more cold nights in the van (I hope not.) But, I am now more confident and positive about my future, because of Sec. 8, and this book I am at the library writing and typing, daily.

I will get to my goal, it just takes time, energy, and patience, which is extremely important if you wish to advance in life, because everything is not going to go your way as quickly as you may think. And if you can't wait, unless God has immediate plans for you, you can lose what little you gained.

I'm more confident now than ever, because I hung in there and didn't give up on what I wanted, in spite of everything going on around me. Praying to God and him delivering, made me more energized, and strengthened my positive desires and way of thinking . . . AMEN?! It's important that I get an apartment as-soon-as-possible so I can get my boys back, and help them in their lives directly, instead of being on a distance and talking by phone. I have less of an effect on their lives living that way. I am still there for them and communicating, especially with the two eldest. They are old enough whereas I don't have to involve their mother in most of the thing involving them. I am very much still into their school work, and whether or not there is progress at school . . . how they are behaving and are they cutting class?

I'm not in their lives directly at this time, the way I would like to be, due to my issues I presently have. I still see them but not as-much-as I would like to. They presently live in the Bronx, in an area that I'm not too cool with. I worry about them daily, and really, they want to be with their dad.

Their mother's boyfriend who just got there, wants to dictate what goes on concerning my sons, and tell them what, when, and who. I get ticked because he's new, like a month new.

He's like his woman, unreasonable. I tried talking with him on the phone, in which he didn't give me a chance to get a word in edge wise. Then I met him face-to-face, where he was even more difficult and sneaky. He's not a smart person through my observation. I know . . . it's what the mother allows. I let her have it as well; she knows I am not a nice person when it comes to my boys. Lots of people think because you're a man you will tolerate more pertaining to the kids, because of our nature. I learned that in the shelter, and going up to their school.

Women don't mess with other women; they stay at a distance from each other, especially when it comes to their children. A large percentage of women will hit the ceiling when it comes to their child (ren), and their child will be dead wrong.

Men don't get bent out of shape and emotional, and begin bitching over miscellaneous nonsense. So certain women feel that they can be sneaky and say and do as they please because they know that a man's nature is not to snap back at minor things. And many women will take advantage of that.

So, with the issues that my sons are going through with their mother (and company), my efforts are on getting them out of the Bronx . . . period!

I tell my boys to call me if they are having any problems with the child adults. They were raised by me and are not used to that level of confusion by their mother; she really takes things over the edge.

They have called me on certain occasions, or, I would call them at the right time they were having problems in the house, with whomever. I would calm them down over the phone first, and then tell them how to handle the situation.

I could hear in their voices when they were finished absorbing my input that they were relaxed, confident, and grateful I was there for them. That's what kids are missing today. Talk, instructions, and directions, on how to act in this lopsided world.

My boys needed direction towards their mother and her friend, which in turn prevented them from getting frustrated, which can lead to other serious issues. My eldest sons called me one day and said he had a problem with his mother's man, and how the mother would jump on her man's side over his. The police were called and at 12 midnight, with the mother having asked my son to leave, even though her man started the commotion, I was told. My son had to leave the Bronx and come way to Queens by train that late, or, that early, whatever way you want to put it.

Listen, if I say things against these women, it's because it's true, not just to bash them to make them look bad, and me look good, No!

When a problem arose concerning my boys, I would let them know what to do. In the beginning they wouldn't listen, but I guess they got tired of certain things and then took my advice. There were times I would look for an apartment and bring them with me on school days, and then send them home after wards. I try to spend as much time with them until my apartment came through.

With God by my side that's just what happened, I found an apartment in Queens and informed my boys about it. I was still homeless, living day-to-day, being patient with life, but at the same time trying to make things happen for my sons and I, and thank God things fell in place. It took months-and-months for it to occur, but with payer, patience, and effort, I began to see the light and thank the lord for being there for me and blessing me with his love, no matter what my situation, **"I LOVE YOU DEEPLY JEHOVAH,"** I do. God bless everyone, remember folks . . . . talk to God, he loves you!

This ladies and gentlemen is my grandmother the amazing woman who just about single handily raised 12 kids on her own, she is my heart, and I loved her tremendously. May the lord be with her as we move forward to the future. She is always in my though . . . I love you Dearly Ma!

This book talks about a man (Me) raising three babies in the N.Y.C. shelter system (A unique story). My goal with this book is not just to educate people on what's happening in the shelter system but to get more fathers of the world to be dedicated to the life that was brought forth by them (I speak to teens and fathers as well about being fathers, I focus on males most.) For more information call or email me me at:

1(347)-969-1080
or
E-@ persistantnow@yahoo.com

Conclusion

I wrote this book to try and make a difference in the lives of the extremely unfortunate which for me are the homeless families and teenagers who were put in a situation they did not ask for, and unlike homeless families, teens in many cases have no strong family, abandoned in a very unfair world. All teens in that predicament, this book is written to encourage, enlighten and direct the young minds. That's who I love and care for. They are our future and deserve better, in order to make a better world, my heart goes out to our young adults, it's their world. I hope they learn from my experiences, I feel obligated to give back.